THE UNIVERSITY OF CHICAGO

ORIENTAL INSTITUTE NUBIAN EXPEDITION

VOLUME IV

EXCAVATIONS BETWEEN ABU SIMBEL AND THE SUDAN FRONTIER

NEOLITHIC, A-GROUP, AND POST-A-GROUP REMAINS

FROM

CEMETERIES W, V, S, Q, T, AND A CAVE EAST OF

CEMETERY K

CAMPAGNE INTERNATIONALE POUR LA SAUVEGARDE
DES MONUMENTS DE LA NUBIE

THE UNIVERSITY OF CHICAGO
ORIENTAL INSTITUTE NUBIAN EXPEDITION
VOLUME IV

Excavations Between Abu Simbel and the Sudan Frontier
KEITH C. SEELE, *Director*

PARTS 2, 3, AND 4:

NEOLITHIC, A-GROUP, AND POST-A-GROUP REMAINS FROM CEMETERIES W, V, S, Q, T, AND A CAVE EAST OF CEMETERY K

by

BRUCE BEYER WILLIAMS

THE ORIENTAL INSTITUTE OF THE UNIVERSITY OF CHICAGO

CHICAGO • ILLINOIS

Library of Congress Catalog Card Number: 88 - 64070

ISBN: 0–918986–54–0

The Oriental Institute, The University of Chicago

TABLE OF CONTENTS

INTRODUCTION

1. EXCAVATIONS BETWEEN ABU SIMBEL AND THE SUDAN FRONTIER, KEITH C. SEELE,
    DIRECTOR. PART 2: NEOLITHIC REMAINS FROM THE CAVE BEHIND CEMETERY K

2. EXCAVATIONS BETWEEN ABU SIMBEL AND THE SUDAN FRONTIER, KEITH C. SEELE,
    DIRECTOR. PART 3: A-GROUP REMAINS FROM CEMETERIES W, V, S, T, AND Q

LIST OF TABLES

LIST OF FIGURES

LIST OF PLATES

LIST OF TEXT AND REGISTER ABBREVIATIONS

amt.	amount
burn.	burnished
C.	Celsius
ca.	circa
Cairo	Cairo Museum number
car.	carnelian
cyl.	cylinder
dec.	decorated or decoration
deg.	degrees
diam.	diameter
dim.	dimension
dio.	diorite
disc.	discarded
dist.	disturbed
dk.	dark
E	east
Eg. Cs.	Egyptian Coarse
egg.	eggshell
ext.	exterior
fai.	faience
gar.	garnet
gast.	gastropod
geo.	geometric
gl.	glazed
gn.	green
hor.	horizontal
hv.	heavy
inc.	incised
int.	interior
irreg.	irregular
L	left
max.	maximum
N	north
n/a	not available for study
no.	number
obj.	object
OIM	Oriental Institute Museum number
ord.	ordinary

ost.	ostrich
pk.	pink
pt.	paint
ptd.	painted
R	right
rect.	rectangle or rectangular
S	south
samp.	sample
Sud.	Sudanese
Syr.-Pl.	Syro-Palestinian
unc.	uncertain
var.	variety
W	west

BIBLIOGRAPHY

Baumgartel, Elise J.

1960   *The Cultures of Prehistoric Egypt II*. London, New York, and Toronto: Oxford University Press.

Bietak, Manfred

1968   *Studien zur Chronologie der Nubischen C-Gruppe: Ein Beitrag zur Frühgeschichte Unternubiens zwischen 2200 und 1550 vor Chr.* Berichte des Österreichischen Nationalkomitees der UNESCO-Aktion für die Rettung der Nubischen Altertümer, vol. 5. Österreichische Akademie der Wissenschaften, Phil.-Hist. Klasse, Denkschriften, vol. 97. Vienna: Hermann Böhlaus Nachf.

Bietak, Manfred and Engelmayer, Reinhold

1963   *Eine frühdynastische Abri-Siedlung mit Felsbildern aus Sayala-Nubien*. Berichte des Österreichischen Nationalkomitees der UNESCO-Aktion für die Rettung der Nubischen Altertümer, vol. 1. Österreichische Akademie der Wissenschaften, Phil.-Hist. Klasse, Denkschriften, vol. 82. Vienna: Hermann Böhlaus Nachf.

Björkman, Gun and Säve-Söderbergh, Torgny

1972   "Seals and Seal Impressions," pp. 117-18 in H.-Å. Nordström, *Neolithic and A-Group Sites*. Scandinavian Joint Expedition to Sudanese Nubia, vol. 3. Copenhagen, Oslo, and Stockholm: Scandinavian University Books.

Bonnet, Charles

1982   "Les fouilles archéologiques de Kerma (Soudan)," *Genava*, n.s. 30: 29-53.

Brunton, Guy

1937   *Mostagedda and the Tasian Culture*. British Museum Expedition to Middle Egypt, First and Second Years, 1928, 1929. London: Bernard Quaritch.

Brunton, Guy and Caton-Thompson, Gertrude

1928   *The Badarian Civilization and Predynastic Remains near Badari*. British School of
         Archaeology in Egypt and Egyptian Research Account, vol. 46. London: British School of
         Archaeology in Egypt and Bernard Quaritch.

Daumas, François

1960   "Rapport sommaire sur les fouilles executées à Ouadi es-Seboua en Mars 1960," *Bulletin
         de l'Institut Français d'Archéologie Orientale* 60: 185-187.

Davies, P. O. A. L.

1962   "Red and Black Egyptian Pottery," *Journal of Egyptian Archaeology* 48: 19-24.

Davies, W. V.

1987   *Tools and Weapons, I. Axes*. Catalogue of Egyptian Antiquities in the British Museum,
         vol. 7. London: British Museum Publications.

Dunham, Dows

1982   *Excavations at Kerma. Part VI*. Boston: Museum of Fine Arts.

Dreyer, Günter

1986   *Elephantine VIII. Der Tempel der Satet: Die Funde der Frühzeit und des alten Reiches*.
         Deutsches Archäologisches Institut Abteilung Kairo. Archäologisches
         Veröffentlichungen, vol. 39. Mainz am Rhein: Philipp von Zabern.

Eiwanger, Josef

1984   *Merimde-Benisalame I: Die Funde der Urschicht*. Deutsches Archäologisches Institut
         Abteilung Kairo. Archäologisches Veröffentlichungen, vol. 47. Mainz am Rhein: Philipp
         von Zabern.

Emery, W. B.

    1949   *Great Tombs of the First Dynasty I.* Cairo: Government Press.

    1954   *Great Tombs of the First Dynasty II.* London: Egypt Exploration Society.

    1963   "Egypt Exploration Society: Preliminary Report on the Excavation at Buhen, 1962," *Kush* 11: 116-20.

Emery, W. B. and Kirwan, L. P.

    1935   *The Excavations and Survey between Wadi es-Sebua and Adindan 1929-1931.* Service des Antiquités de l'Égypte; Mission Archéologique de Nubie, 1929-1934. Cairo: Government Press, Bulaq.

Firth, C. M.

    1927   *The Archaeological Survey of Nubia, Report for 1910-1911.* Cairo: Government Press.

Fischer, Henry

    1963   "Varia Aegyptiaca," *JARCE* 2: 17-51.

Garstang, John

    1903   *Mahasna and Bet Khallaf.* Egyptian Research Account, vol. 7. London: Bernard Quaritch.

Geus, Francis

    1976   *Rapport annuel d'activité, 1975-1976.* Direction Générale des Antiquités et des Musées Nationaux du Soudan: Section Français de Recherche Archéologique. Khartoum: Khaemi el Gurashi Advertising and Printing.

    1980   *Rapport annuel d'activité, 1978-1979.* Direction Générale des Antiquités et des Musées Nationaux du Soudan: Section Français de Recherche Archéologique. Lille: Université de Lille III.

    1981   *Rapport annuel d'activité, 1979-1980.* Direction Générale des Antiquités et des Musées Nationaux du Soudan: Section Français de Recherche Archéologique. Lille: Université de Lille III.

1983   *Rapport annuel d'activité, 1980-1982.* Direction Générale des Antiquités et des Musées
            Nationaux du Soudan: Section Français de Recherche Archéologique. Lille: Université de
            Lille III.

Geus, Francis and Reinold, Jacques

1979   "Fouille de sauvetage à El Kadada (Soudan): La campagne d'avril, 1976," *Cahier de
            Recherches de l'Institut de Papyrologie et d'Égyptologie de Lille.* No. 5. *Études sur
            l'Égypte et le Soudan anciens.* Lille: Publications de l'Université de Lille III: 7-158.

Hellström, Pontus and Langballe, Hans

1970   *The Rock Drawings.* The Scandinavian Joint Expedition to Sudanese Nubia, vol. 1.
            Copenhagen, Oslo, and Stockholm: Scandinavian University Books.

Helck, Wolfgang

1987   *Untersuchungen zur Thinitenzeit.* Ägyptologische Abhandlungen, vol. 45. Wiesbaden:
            Otto Harrassowitz.

Hofmann, Inge

1967   *Die Kulturen des Niltals von Aswan bis Sennar vom Mesolithikum bis zum Ende der
            christlichen Epoche.* Monographien zur Völkerkunde, vol. 4. Hamburg:
            Kommissionverlag Cram de Gruyter and Co.

Holthoer, Rostislav

1977   *New Kingdom Pharaonic Sites: The Pottery.* The Scandinavian Joint Expedition to
            Sudanese Nubia, vol. 5:1. Copenhagen, Oslo, and Stockholm: Scandinavian University
            Books.

Kaiser, Werner

1985a   "Zur Südausdehnung der vorgeschichtlichen Deltakulturen und zur frühen Entwicklung
            Oberägyptens," *MDAIK* 41: 61-87.

1985b   "Zu Entwicklung und Vorformen der frühzeitlichen Gräber mit reich gegleiderter
            Oberbaufassade," pp. 25-38 in *Mélanges Gamal eddin Mokhtar*, vol. 2. Cairo: Institut
            Français d'Archéologie Orientale du Caire.

Kaiser, Werner and Dreyer, Günter

    1982   "Nachuntersuchungen im frühzeitlichen Königsfriedhof 2. Vorbericht," *MDAIK* 38: 211-

Kaiser, Werner; Dreyer, Günter; Gempeler, Robert; Grossmann, Peter; Haeny, Gerhard; Jaritz, Horst; and
    Junge, Friedrich

    1976   "Stadt und Tempel von Elephantine Sechster Grabungsbericht," *MDAIK* 32: 67-112.

Kaiser, Werner; Dreyer, Günter; Gempeler, Robert; Grossmann, Peter; and Jaritz, Horst

    1977   "Stadt und Tempel von Elephantine Siebter Grabungsbericht," *MDAIK* 33: 63-100.

Kantor, Helene J.

    1948   "Oriental Institute Museum Notes: A Predynastic Ostrich Egg with Incised Decoration,"
             JNES 7: 46-51.

Lecointe, Yves

    1987   "Le site néolithique d'el Ghaba: Deux années d'activité (1985-1986)," *Archéologie du Nil*
             Moyen 2: 69-87.

Lilyquist, Christine

    1971   "Ancient Egyptian Mirrors from the Earliest Times through the Middle Kingdom." Ph.D.
             Dissertation, New York University.

    1979   *Ancient Egyptian Mirrors from the Earliest Times through the Middle Kingdom.*
             Münchner Ägyptologische Studien, vol. 27. Munich: Deutscher Kunstverlag.

Mayer-Thurman, Christa and Williams, Bruce

    1979   *Ancient Textiles from Nubia.* Chicago: The Art Institute of Chicago and The Oriental
             Institute of The University of Chicago.

Merpert, N. Y. and Bolshakov, O. G.

    1964   "Rannedinasticheskoe Poseienie Khor-Daud," pp. 83-177 in *Drevnai͡a Nubia.* Ed. B.B.
             Piotrovsky. Moscow: Akademii͡a Nauk.

Myers, O. H.

    1958   "Abka Re-excavated," *Kush* 6: 131-41.

    1960   "Abka Again," *Kush* 8: 174-81.

Nordström, Hans-Åke

    1972   *Neolithic and A-Group Sites*. The Scandinavian Joint Expedition to Sudanese Nubia, vol. 3. Copenhagen, Oslo, and Stockholm: Scandinavian University Books.

O'Connor, David

    1986   "The Locations of Yam and Kush and Their Historical Implications," *JARCE* 23: 27-50.

Oren, Eliezer

    1973   "The Overland Route between Egypt and Canaan in the Early Bronze Age (Preliminary Report)," *Israel Exploration Journal* 23: 198-205.

Petrie, W. M. Flinders

    1901   *The Royal Tombs of the Earliest Dynasties. 1901. Part II*. Egypt Exploration Fund Memoir 21. London: Egypt Exploration Fund.

    1917   *Tools and Weapons*. British School of Archaeology in Egypt and Egyptian Research Account, vol. 30. London: British School of Archaeology in Egypt and Constable and Co. and Bernard Quaritch.

    1920   *Prehistoric Egypt*. British School of Archaeology in Egypt and Egyptian Research Account, vol. 31. London: British School of Archaeology in Egypt and Bernard Quaritch.

    1921   *Corpus of Prehistoric Pottery and Palettes*. British School of Archaeology in Egypt and Egyptian Research Account, vol. 32. London: British School of Archaeology in Egypt and Constable and Co. and Bernard Quaritch.

Petrie, W. M. Flinders and Quibell, J. E.

    1896   *Naqada and Ballas. 1895*. Egyptian Research Account, vol. 1. London: Bernard Quaritch.

Reinold, Jacques

    1987   "Les fouilles pré- et proto-historiques de la Section Française de la Direction des Antiquités du Soudan: Les campagnes 1984-85 et 1985-86," *Archéologie du Nil moyen* 2:

Reisner, G. A.

    1910   *The Archaeological Survey of Nubia, Report for 1907-1908*, vol. 1. Cairo: National Printing Department.

    1942   *A History of the Giza Necropolis*, vol. 1. Cambridge: Harvard University Press.

    1955   *A History of the Giza Necropolis*, vol. 2 (completed by W. S. Smith). Cambridge: Harvard University Press.

Seele, Keith C.

    1974   "University of Chicago Oriental Institute Nubian Expedition: Excavations between Abu Simbel and the Sudan Border, Preliminary Report," *JNES* 33: 1-43.

Shiner, Joel

    1968   "The Cataract Tradition," pp. 535-629 in Fred Wendorff et al. *The Prehistory of Nubia*, vol. 2. Dallas: Fort Burgwin Research Center and Southern Methodist University Press, 1968.

Smith, H. S.

    1962   *Preliminary Reports of the Egypt Exploration Society's Nubian Survey*. Cairo: General Organization for Government Printing Offices.

    1966   "The Nubian B-Group," *Kush* 14: 69-124.

Stadelmann, Rainer

    1985   "Die Oberbauten der Königsgräber der 2. Dynastie in Saqqara," pp. 295-307 in *Mélanges Gamal eddin Mokhtar*, vol. 2. Cairo: Institut Français d'Archéologie Orientale du Caire.

Steindorff, Georg

    1935   *Aniba, Erster Band*. Glückstadt and Hamburg: J. J. Augustin.

Tobert, Natalie

    1984   "Ethnoarchaeology of pottery firing in Darfur, Sudan: implications for ceramic technology studies," *Oxford Journal of Archaeology* 3: 141-56.

Trigger, Bruce G.

    1965   *History and Settlement in Nubia.* Yale University Publications in Anthropology, no. 69. New Haven: Department of Anthropology, Yale University.

Vila, André

    1979   *La prospection archéologique de la vallée du Nil au sud de la cataracte de Dal (Nubie soudanaise). Fascicule 11: Récapitulations et conclusions, appendices.* Paris: Centre Nationale de la Recherche Scientifique.

    1980   *La prospection archéologique de la vallée du Nil au sud de la cataracte de Dal (Nubie soudanaise). Fascicule 12: La nécropole de Missiminia I, les sépultures napatéennes.* Paris: Centre Nationale de la Recherche Scientifique.

Vinogradov, A. V.

    1964   "Raskopki mogil'nikov v rayone sel. zapadnaĭa Koshtamna," pp. 205-28 in *Drevnaĭa Nubia.* Ed. B. B. Piotrovsky. Moscow: Akademiĭa Nauk.

Wendorff, Fred

    1968   "Site 117: A Nubian Final Paleolithic Graveyard near Gebel Sahaba, Sudan," pp. 954-95 in *The Prehistory of Nubia.* Ed. Fred Wendorff. Dallas: Fort Burgwin Research Center and Southern Methodist University Press.

Wendorff, Fred and Schild, Romuald et al.

    1980   *Prehistory of the Eastern Sahara.* New York, London, Toronto, Sydney, and San Francisco: Academic Press.

    1984   *Cattle-Keepers of the Eastern Sahara: The Neolithic of Bir Kiseiba.* Ed. Angela E. Close. Dallas: Department of Anthropology, Southern Methodist University.

Williams, Bruce

 1982 "Notes on Prehistoric Cache Fields of Lower Egyptian Tradition at Sedment," *JNES* 41: 213-21.

 1985 "A Chronology of Meroitic Occupation below the Fourth Cataract," *JARCE* 22: 149-95.

 1987 "Forebears of Menes in Nubia: Myth or Reality?," *JNES* 46: 15-26.

 1988 *Painted Pottery and the Art of Naqada III.* Münchner Ägyptologische Studien, vol. 45. Munich: Deutscher Kunstverlag.

Williams, Bruce and Logan, Thomas J.

 1987 "The Metropolitan Museum Knife Handle and Aspects of Pharaonic Imagery before Narmer," *JNES* 46: 245-85.

LIST OF BIBLIOGRAPHICAL ABBREVIATIONS

JARCE	*Journal of the American Research Center in Egypt*, New York.
Kush	*Kush*, Journal of the Sudan Antiquities Service, Khartoum.
JNES	*Journal of Near Eastern Studies*, Chicago.
MDAIK	*Mitteilungen des Deutschen Archäologischen Instituts Abteilung Kairo*, Mainz am Rhein.
OINE III	Bruce Williams, *Excavations between Abu Simbel and the Sudan Frontier, Keith C. Seele, Director. Part 1: The A-Group Royal Cemetery at Qustul: Cemetery L.* Oriental Institute Nubian Expedition, vol. III. Chicago: The Oriental Institute of The University of Chicago, 1986.
OINE V	Bruce Williams, *Excavations between Abu Simbel and the Sudan Frontier, Keith C. Seele, Director. Part 5: C-Group, Pan Grave, and Kerma Remains from Adindan Cemeteries T, K, U, and J.* The Oriental Institute Nubian Expedition, vol. V. Chicago: The Oriental Institute of The University of Chicago, 1983.
OINE VII	Bruce Williams, *Excavations between Abu Simbel and the Sudan Frontier, Keith C. Seele, Director. Part 7: Twenty-Fifth Dynasty and Napatan Remains from Qustul Cemeteries W and V.* The Oriental Institute Nubian Expedition, vol. VII. Chicago: The Oriental Institute of the University of Chicago, forthcoming.
OINE IX	Bruce Williams, *Excavations between Abu Simbel and the Sudan Frontier, Keith C. Seele, Director. Part 9: Noubadian X-Group Royal Funerary Complexes and Private Cemeteries at Qustul and Ballana.* The Oriental Institute Nubian Expedition, vol. IX. Chicago: The Oriental Institute of the University of Chicago, forthcoming.
OINE X	Bruce Williams, *Excavations at Serra East, George R. Hughes and James Knudstad, Directors. Parts 1, 2, 3, and 4: A-Group, C-Group, Pan Grave, and New Kingdom Cemeteries.* The Oriental Institute Nubian Expedition, vol. X. Chicago: The Oriental Institute of the University of Chicago, forthcoming.

Dedicated to the memory of Professor Klaus Baer

ACKNOWLEDGEMENTS

The completion of this volume is due to the efforts of many who devoted time and effort to the publication project. Joanna Steinkeller was responsible for most of the drawings, with assistance from Lisa Heidorn (who also assisted with production) and Florence Ovadia, who served as a volunteer. Jean Grant and Ursula Schneider provided prints and photography. Diederika Seele was a constant supporter of the project. Elizabeth Tieken spent many hours repairing pottery, which Karen Bradley carefully organized for storage and to verify recording. Linda Braidwood offered advice on the flints, and stones were identified by Carol Meyer. Important volunteer support was given by Carmen McGarry. The typesetting and page design were carried out by David Baird, and the project owes much to the University of Chicago Computation Center for use of an optical character reader to convert manuscripts. Significant bibliographic assistance was given by Charles Jones, and the author is indebted to Raymond Tindel, Honorio Torres, and James Richerson for many acts of assistance.

The field operations of the Oriental Institute Nubian Expedition between Abu Simbel and the Sudan border were financed from Counterpart Funds in Egypt under United States Department of State Contract 29633. The publication of the series is financed in part by generous assistance from Mr. and Mrs. John W. Leslie and an anonymous donor.

SPECIAL ACKNOWLEDGEMENT

The success of any excavation depends upon the commitment and skill of its leading field staff, who carry out almost all of the observation and recording and manage the daily operations in each area. As in most expeditions of this kind, the staff performed many services other than the functions for which they are listed below. Their months of labor and sacrifice made this publication possible. They deserve special recognition and our deepest gratitude.

	1962-1963	1963-1964
Architects:	James E. Knudstad	Donald D. Bickford
Archaeologists:	Labib Habachi	Carl E. DeVries
	Louis V. Zabkar	Boleslaw Marczuk
	Alfred J. Hoerth	
Photographer:	Otto J. Schaden	
Anthropologist:		Duane Burnor
Registrars:	Sylvia Ericson	Simone Deprez
Inspectors:	Fuad Yakub	Fuad Yakub
		Farouk Gomaa
Foremen:	Hussein el-Sawaq	
	Mohammed Hassan Unweis	

INTRODUCTION

This volume, the second in the series presenting remains found by the Oriental Institute Nubian Expedition between Abu Simbel and the Sudan Frontier, includes materials of Neolithic, A-Group, and late Archaic or Old Kingdom date not found in the Royal Cemetery (Cemetery L). Because of their special importance, the unique materials from Cemetery L have been given separate treatment in *OINE* III. However, it is very much a companion volume, and detailed discussions of classification and comparanda found there are only referred to and not repeated here.

Early remains were found in the entire area explored by the Oriental Institute Nubian Expedition from Cemetery T at Adindan to Cemetery Q, the great cemetery of X-Group times. Almost all the early remains were from the A-Group period. There was one Neolithic site, a cave in the high rock behind Cemetery K, and two tombs in Cemetery T contained material that probably was contemporary with the later Archaic and Old Kingdom period in Egypt.

All the sites, except the cave, were found on the low desert terrace immediately behind the cultivated area. Except for Cemetery W,[1] the graves were not found in cemeteries but in small clusters containing a few A-Group burials, generally near or in between tombs of a later date. Sometimes, the early burials were so sparsely scattered among densely-packed later tombs that plans made for the present work could not include the entire cemetery. Instead, the early burials are shown on a plan of part of the cemetery (key plan), either alone or with a few added special details, such as important later tombs, houses, or the boundaries of the cemetery. These details locate the places with early tombs on key plans that show the locations of these areas in relation to the larger outlines of the cemeteries (pls. 2-7) shown on the concession map itself (pl. 1). A complete plan of one compact A-Group cemetery, W1, is given. Since a complete plan of Cemetery T has been published,[2] no key plan of that cemetery is included here.

NOTES

1. Cemetery W consists of two areas designated by Seele as W1 and W2 and presented by him in 1974, fig. 1. They are not to be confused with tomb numbers, which are spaced throughout, for example, W 1, W 11, etc.
2. *OINE* V, pl. 2.

1

EXCAVATIONS BETWEEN ABU SIMBEL AND THE SUDAN FRONTIER

KEITH C. SEELE, DIRECTOR. PART 2:

NEOLITHIC REMAINS FROM THE CAVE BEHIND CEMETERY K

The earliest materials excavated by the Oriental Institute Nubian Expedition were found in a cave east of Cemetery K. Although the cave was not surveyed properly or excavated in a stratigraphically controlled manner, the materials seem to be consistent enough to be considered contemporary with each other.

A. DESCRIPTION OF THE CAVE

The cave was located in a prominent outcrop in the south face of the *khor*, about 15 m from its bottom and 1.5 m from the top of the gebel. Above it, on the promontory, were stone circles thought to be C-Group.[1] Access to the cave was restricted by blocklike slabs of sandstone (fig. 1a, b). Behind them, a narrow oval chamber extended diagonally 2.80 × ca. 1.50 × 1.80 m; behind it was a high, deep shelf located only .40 m below the ceiling. Almost 2.50 m deep, this shelf, or loculus, curved sharply around the end of the cave away from the doorway. Ridges on it were reported but not clearly described in the record. However, a characteristic ancient method of cutting rooms in rock was to carve a shallow shelf backwards at ceiling height, cut parallel grooves in it, and break up the protruding ridges with large stone hammers, alternating these procedures until the desired floor level was reached. Because the remains from this cave are so early and the cave itself was described in a very summary fashion in the records, it would be difficult to show that it was completely or partly artificial, but the cave's shape and the grooved shelf are even more difficult to explain as being purely natural.

B. POTTERY

The few (thirty-two) sherds found in the cave correspond rather closely to pottery described by Nordström as Abkan,[2] and they can be assigned to approximately six groups according to the materials and processes used in making them (table 1).[3]

3

a. MATERIALS AND PROCESSES IN ABKAN POTTERY

CLAY

No significant difference could be observed between the clay used to make these vessels and that described in Abkan pottery found elsewhere, although the mica Nordström reported in fabrics from Sudan near the cataract was not prominent in this pottery, and it would appear that a local silty clay was used.[4]

TEMPER

Observable inclusions were mostly particles of sand (with some carnelian) of different sizes up to one millimeter. There were a few irregular voids left by organic matter, possibly indicating the presence of soil. Some very crumbly sherds of one group have a greyish, spongy texture with angular carbon fragments which indicate that ash was used.

SHAPING

From the few rims present, it appears that the vessels were almost all simple bowls with straight, vertical, or angled sides and smooth contours. There are no carinations or abrupt curves, and most body sherds are nearly flat. Most of the rims are beveled, as are those of most comparable A-Group bowls.[5] The smoothness of the profile seems to indicate that this pottery was made by the same method used to make A-Group pottery, that is, the clay was pressed against the ground,[6] but one sherd from Form Group I has an irregular surface, indicating that it was pinched, or modeled, by hand from a lump of clay.

SURFACE

Except in the case of Form Group I vessels, all of the surfaces had been burnished evenly to a low luster, and a few were rippled. The rippled surfaces have relatively broad facets rather than the short, narrow grooves commonly found on A-Group rippled pottery. Sherds from Form Group I were scraped or smoothed on the inside.

DECORATION

One rim sherd from Form Group I was decorated with groups of pendant, incised triangles below the rim and rows of rectangular impressions below these triangles.

COATING

Sherds from Form Group II were given a red exterior coat.

FIRING

Although the sherds are hard enough to be considered completely fired, they do not resist breaking well, and the sherds of pottery tempered with ash crumble readily. Nordström estimated that the pottery was fired for a relatively short time at about 500 to 700° C. in an atmosphere that was oxidizing or neutral.[7] Actually, the atmosphere was variable, and areas of fire blooms and smudges appear on the surfaces.

POST-FIRING TREATMENT

Most of the vessels in other groups and a few in Form Group I have black interior surfaces,[8] possibly due to a secondary firing technique described elsewhere. Almost all of the red-coated vessels, however, were not blackened inside.

Although there were only thirty-two sherds in the collection, two, each from different groups, had evidently been repaired; this was indicated by the holes bored into them.

b. THE CLASSIFICATION OF ABKAN POTTERY FROM THE CAVE

The small size of the collection hardly permits comprehensive classification. As with A-Group pottery, the intentional categories appear to have permitted variations in interior color despite the fact that exterior color and surface treatment are the most strongly developed features of the pottery and the bases for classifying it. The following outline is a tentative classification by Form Group. The uppercase letters under the Form Groups indicate individual vessels within the Form Group rather than types. Colors are noted in parentheses according to the Munsell Soil Color Charts.

Table 1 — Pottery from the Cave East of Cemetery K

Form Group I. Coarse Pottery, scraped or smoothed (pl. 12a).[a]

    A. K-Cave — 6, 1 sherd: bowl rim, hand modeled, scraped; decoration of nested, incised pendant triangles at the rim, rows of square impressions below (fig. 2d).

    B. K-Cave — 7, 5 sherds: bowl rim and body smoothed, black on both sides (also brown, 10YR 5/3, fig. 2c).

    C. K-Cave — 8, 2 sherds: body, wiped exterior, smoothed interior, buff exterior, black interior (10YR 5/2, 10YR 6/4).

Form Group II. Red-Coated (pl. 12b).[b]

    A. K-Cave — 9, 4 sherds: burnished red coat, both sides, evenly fired (10R 5/6).

    B. K-Cave — 10, 4 sherds: red exterior, grey-buff interior, crumbling (2.5YR 6/4, 10YR 5/3).

    C. K-Cave — 11, 4 sherds: 2 rims; red/mottled grey exterior, tan-buff interior (2.5YR 5/6, 10YR 6/2, fig. 2a).

Form Group III. Black Burnished (pl. 12c).[c]

    A. K-Cave — 12, 1 sherd: bowl rim, black polished inside and out; three holes for repair (fig 2b).

Form Group IV. Dark Brown and Black Burnished (pl. 12c).[d]

    A. K-Cave — 13, 2 sherds: thin bowl, very dark exterior, black interior (black and 10YR 5/3).

    B. K-Cave — 14, 5 sherds: interior greyish (5YR 3/2 to grey, light areas 10YR 7/2).

    C. K-Cave — 15, 1 sherd: ash-tempered (5YR 3/2).

Form Group V. Rippled (pl. 12d).[e]

    A. K-Cave — 16, 2 sherds (5YR 3/2 to grey, 10YR 6/4).

Uncertain: K-Cave — 5.

---

[a]Nordström 1972, pp. 58-59. This group corresponds approximately to Nordström's Ware M 1.01 and M 1.02, coarse and scraped Abkan wares.

[b]No red-coated Abkan pottery without a black interior is recognized in Nordström's classification, but the difference is only in the omission of the step that produced the blackening (Nordström 1972, p. 60; see M 4.11 and M 4.12).

[c]This group corresponds to Nordström's ware-group M 3 (3.01), burnished black Abkan wares (1972, p. 59).

[d]This group corresponds to Nordström's (1972, p. 59) wares M 4.01 (burnished brown and black Abkan ware) and M 2.01 (burnished brown Abkan ware).

[e]This particular pair of sherds would have been classed with Nordström's ware M 4.02 (also M 2.02 and M 4.12), although he recognized other color combinations which would have been assigned to this group had they been found here, including brown, brown with black interior, and red with black interior. Because few shapes are preserved anywhere, the classification is inevitably tentative, but it should be pointed out that the most readily detectable difference in this pottery is between various treatments of the surface. Both classifications probably contain too many categories. It is more likely that only three major categories that deserved the status of "wares" existed in Abkan pottery, each with a number of possible color combinations.

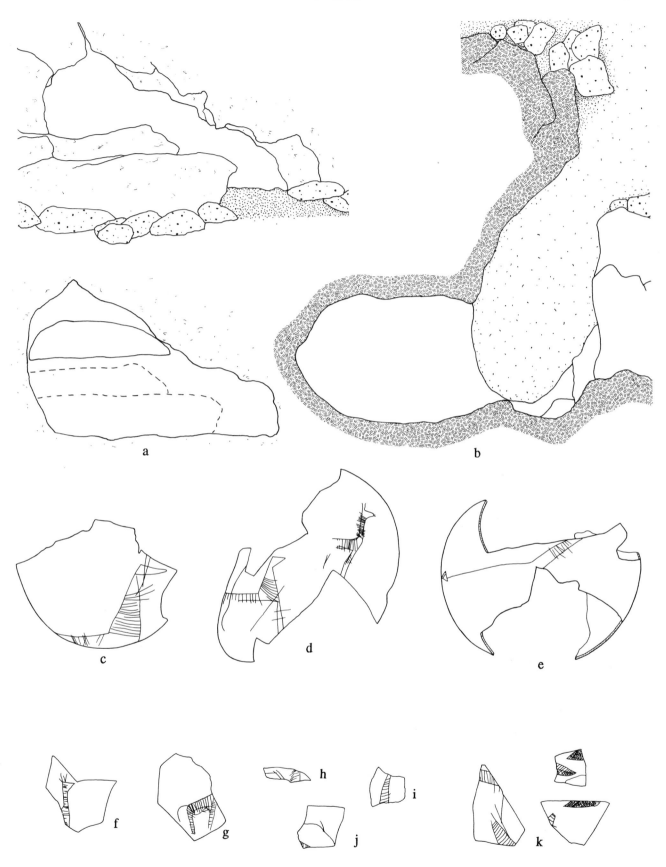

Figure 1. The cave east of Cemetery K: (a) External view and vertical section; (b) Plan; Ostrich egg fragments — (c-e) A; (f) B; (g) C; (h) D; (i) G; (j) E; (k) E; (k) F. Scale 2:5 except (a) 1:50.

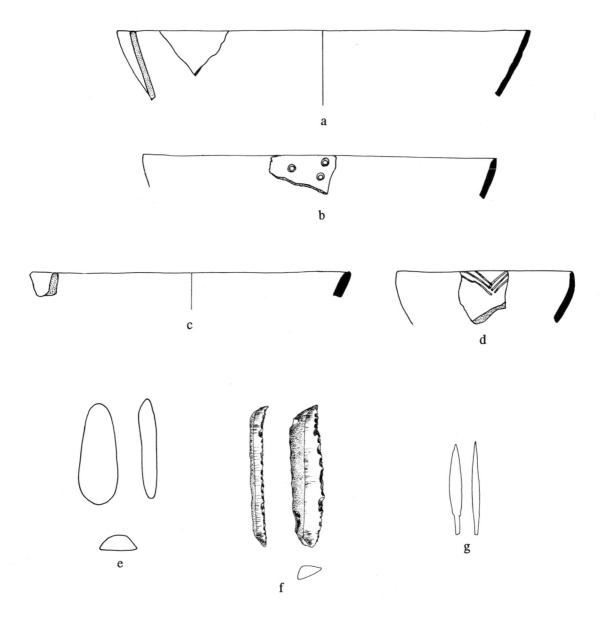

Figure 2. The cave east of Cemetery K, pottery and objects: Red-Coated pottery, Form Group II— (a) C; Black Polished pottery, Form Group III— (b) A; Coarse pottery, Form Group I— (c) B; (d) A; (e) Pebble, no. 5; (f) Stone tool, no. 2; (g) Bone point or tool, no. 3. Scale 2:5.

C. OBJECTS

The objects from this cave include part of the skull of a small, horned animal (K-Cave — 1, pl. 13a), a cortex-backed flint blade with denticulate retouch (K-Cave — 2, fig. 2f, pl. 13a),[9] a simple bone borer (K-Cave — 3, fig. 2g, pl. 13a), gourd fragments (K-Cave — 4), a pebble (K-Cave — 5, fig. 2e, pl. 13a), and ostrich eggshell fragments, many of which were decorated (K-Cave — 18-23 and fourteen unplaced fragments).

By far, the most important objects found in the cave are the incised ostrich eggshell fragments (table 2). These were decorated with very simple, light, and often almost invisible designs of animals and other shapes filled in with hatching and crosshatching. The most common representations are giraffes, shown with rectangular bodies and upright necks (in Naqada I painting, and in rock drawings, the back is normally shown by a straight line from the rump to the head).[10] The horns and sometimes the mane are shown. Other shapes cannot be distinguished, but floating, crosshatched lozenges resemble similar shapes incised on an ostrich egg in the Oriental Institute.[11]

In addition to the objects in the collection, the records indicate that a number of other "flake tools" and the skull of an adult female were also found.

Table 2 — Fragments of Ostrich Eggshell

Locus and object no.	Remarks
K-Cave — 17	Egg, ca. 1/2-2/3 of surface remains, parts of three giraffes, and part of uncertain shape (fig. 1c-e; pls. 8, 9, 10a).
K-Cave — 18	Fragment, probably not part of A; giraffe, head to shoulder (fig. 1f; pl. 10b, 11e).
K-Cave — 19	Fragment, giraffe from neck down (fig. 1g; pl. 10b, 11d).
K-Cave — 20	Giraffe, part of neck; fragment (fig. 1h; pl. 11a).
K-Cave — 21	Giraffe, neck; fragment (fig. 1j; pl 10b, 11b).
K-Cave — 22	Three fragments; lozenges, hatched and crosshatched, deeply cut (fig. 1k; pl. 10c, 11f-h).
K-Cave — 23	Uncertain; band shape, hatched; fragment (fig. 1i; pl. 11c).
K-Cave — 24	Fourteen fragments, some with scratches.

D. CONCLUSION: THE CAVE AT ADINDAN AND EARLY CAVE OR CLEFT SHRINES IN NUBIA AND EGYPT

If indeed an occurrence of Abkan, the cave east of Cemetery K is the northernmost site at which remains of this culture have been found and published, although it is not far north of the Faras site.[12] Perhaps the most remarkable feature of this culture is the sparseness of settlement, which contrasts with the much denser settlement of A-Group in the same areas.[13] Two significant features of the cave site are noteworthy: one is the group of incised eggshells discussed above,[14] and the second is the structure of the cave itself. Although the photograph indicates that the blocks of stone in front of the cave were not installed intentionally (pl. 45), it would appear that the structure of the cave was modifed, for the grooves in the cave's interior shelf were probably cut.

The cave may be compared with the so-called shelter settlement at Sayala, which included one shelter with a walled-off entrance and complexes of rock drawings on the ceiling. Although remains of fire-pits were found, the debris with bones and vessels found in these shelters was hardly of the type associated with settlements. Ostrich eggshells and two Naqada II/Gerzean sandstone (!) lug-handled vessels would indicate a more specialized use.[15]

Major stages in a sequence of development may be found in the early levels of the archaic Satet Temple at Elephantine. At first, this was hardly more than a grotto containing votive objects with a wall in front of it. In time, these structures became increasingly complex, and they were finally replaced by a substantial, free-standing temple.[16]

Despite apparent differences between the Abkan and A-Group cultures, the Qustul and Sayala caves were almost or actually contemporary, and the early Satet Temple, located in a region that had been occupied by A-Group, was in use only very shortly afterward. The geographical and chronological proximity of these caves or grottos suggests a relationship, one also suggested by the rock-drawing traditions shared by both Nubia and Upper Egypt.

Table 3 — Register of Finds from the Cave

Object	Table reference	Field category
1. Fragment of gazelle (?) skull		samp.
2. Flint blade		samp.
3. Bone borer		samp.
4. Fragments of gourd		samp.
5. Pebble		samp.
6. Sherd, Form Group I	1	sherd
7. Sherds, Form Group I	1	sherds
8. Sherds, Form Group I	1	sherds
9. Sherds, Form Group II	1	sherds
10. Sherds, Form Group II	1	sherds
11. Sherds, Form Group II	1	sherds
12. Sherd, Form Group III	1	sherd
13. Sherds, Form Group IV	1	sherds
14. Sherds, Form Group IV	1	sherds
15. Sherd, Form Group IV	1	sherd
16. Sherds, Form Group V	1	sherds
17. Ostrich egg	2	samp.
18. Ostrich egg fragment	2	samp.
19. Ostrich egg fragment	2	samp.
20. Ostrich egg fragment	2	samp.
21. Ostrich egg fragment	2	samp.
22. Ostrich egg fragments	2	samp.
23. Ostrich egg fragment	2	samp.
24. Fourteen Ostrich egg fragments		
25. Skull of adult female		disc.
26. Uncertain number of flake tools		disc.

NOTES

1. Smith 1962, p. 9, cem. 229. Some were certainly later C-Group (*OINE* V, Appendix). Smith also noted (ibid.) rock shelters with nearby drawings directly behind Adindan. Although some of these may have been C-Group, his description and photographs taken by the Oriental Institute Nubian Expedition indicate many were A-Group and earlier. For general discussions of the Neolithic in the area, see Nordström 1972, pp. 6-17, and Wendorff and Schild et al. 1984, conclusion.

2. Nordström 1972, pp. 57-60, 47-50.

3. *OINE* III, pp. 191-95.

4. Nordström 1972, p. 49.

5. Beveled, bulged, and milled rims are characteristic of pottery in the Sudanese Neolithic of the cataract region (Nordström 1972, pls. 141, 1-3; 123: 1, 2, 8, 31; 122: 3, 4, 8). Larger bowls and burnished jars tend to have beveled or milled rims in A-Group pottery (*OINE* III, fig. 24e; see pp. 22 below).

6. See *OINE* III, p. 23, figs. 2-3. See also Tobert 1984, pp. 143-44 for shaping techniques in modern Darfur.

7. Nordström 1972, p. 49. Although not discussed in detail by Nordström, smudging and fire blooms are found on many of these sherds and on most ordinary A-Group pottery. See also Tobert 1984, pp. 145-46 and 153-54 for firing temperatures now in use in Darfur. Note, however that mineral tempers occur in the Abkan, while Darfur clays require a good deal of organic inclusions to survive the firing process.

8. *OINE* III, p. 25; *OINE* V, p. 39, note 24. Tobert (1984, pp. 145) reports a way of achieving a blackened interior in a single firing. Depending on the shape of the vessel, it is placed in the firing pit either mouth down or mouth up, flush with the ground. The method is somewhat different from that tried experimentally by P. Davies (1962).

9. Although backed blades are rather uncommon in Abkan (Randi Håland, "Lithic Artifacts" in Nordström 1972, p. 95), cortex is often used, and the object that most resembles this tool is a scraper from site 2002 (Early Abkan, Shiner 1968, fig. 44 t, p. 613; see also pp. 625-27).

10. Hellström and Langballe 1970, Corpus K. Giraffes with necks at an angle to the back do occur as in K 60-74, 104. See also, Petrie 1920, pl. XVIII: 73.

11. Kantor 1948. The ovals are discussed on p. 51. Divided ovals have been interpreted as vulvae (Hellström 1970, Corpus AA: 9–16), but they may be giraffe hoof prints as depicted recently in Sudan. The band with hatching (23G) also appears on an ostrich egg fragment from Khor Daud (Merpert and Bolshakov, 1964, p. 174, fig. 65).

12. For a list of sites in northernmost Sudan and a mention of possible occurrences in Lower Nubia, see Nordström 1972, pp. 12-13.

13. This is documented by such details as the beveled bowl rims. See above, note 5.

14. As portable two-dimensional representations, they are unique in the Neolithic of Nubia and Sudan as it occurs in and near the Nile Valley itself.

15. Bietak and Engelmayer 1963. For the structures of the rock shelters, see plans 1-2, pls. I-III and IV-IX; rock-drawings are on plan 3 and pls. XX-XXXV, XXXVI-XXXVII. The stone jars are illustrated on pl. 14: 1-2, 17 (see p. 12). For another rock-shelter with painted decoration, see Smith 1962, pp. 79-90. See also Daumas 1960. In the Scandinavian concession, rock drawings were concentrated in the rocky area at the cataract itself (Hellström and Langballe 1970), where they occurred most often within bays (map 15, 160a, with a structured access?) or on the face of a rocky eminence. Many were made in A-Group, as indicated by the types of barks represented (see Williams and Logan 1987, Appendix B). Rock-clefts in this area, some with drawings, all with evidence of early occupation are detailed by Nordström 1972. See pp. 222-23 and pl. 130, Farki site 408 area 1 (with Abkan and other pottery); p. 279 and pl. 135, Abka site 424 (pothole with rock drawings, no pottery); and especially p. 233 and pl. 135, Abka site 378g (called site 387, with rock drawings, Abkan and other pottery).

16. Dreyer 1986, especially pp. 11-22; Kaiser et al. 1976, pp. 68-87, especially pp. 75-87; and Kaiser et al. 1977, pp. 64-83. See also Dreyer 1986, especially pp. 18-20 and figs. 9-18, for the sequence of architectural phases and deposits. Deposits of concretions, quartz pebbles, and ostrich eggshells are discussed on pp. 96-97 and listed on p. 153.

2

EXCAVATIONS BETWEEN ABU SIMBEL AND THE SUDAN FRONTIER

KEITH C. SEELE, DIRECTOR. PART 3:

A-GROUP REMAINS FROM CEMETERIES W, V, S, T, AND Q

A-Group material was found in five areas other than Cemetery L and included several different types of locus. All of the A-Group sites were on the low desert terrace near or below the 123-m contour (above sea level, also known as river level), the maximum normal height of water behind the old Aswan Dam after its second raising. Four shafts in Cemetery S may have been part of the Cemetery L complexes. The other locations consisted of one cemetery (W 1) and scattered groups, isolated tombs, and caches, including a number found among the late tombs in Cemetery Q. Excluding Cemetery L, the tombs and other loci with numbers amounted to just over one hundred and the approximately thirty unnumbered pits in Cemetery W. However, A-Group deposits appear to be more scattered and sparse than they probably originally were, since much of the area in which A-Group tombs and deposits were made was later covered with modern houses and could not be excavated.

A-Group remains were least disturbed in Cemetery W 1. The condition of the tombs was consistently better than any other A-Group loci found by the expedition. The present-day village of Qustul never covered the area, and there was relatively little plundering; many of the tombs were untouched before excavation. The expedition assigned numbers primarily to tombs, although many cache pits, most of which were circular, were found in Cemetery W.

The area along the low desert terrace called Cemetery V actually comprised several clusters, including a few scattered clusters of A-Group burials, isolated burials, and circular cache pits, some of which had been reused for burials. Cemetery S was a small area containing five New Kingdom graves and four A-Group deposit shafts, which were contemporary with Cemetery L and probably connected to it as part of a cemetery-complex. Cemetery T, the very large C-Group cemetery (see *OINE* V), contained a number of poor, scattered A-Group burials. Four areas in Cemetery Q (which contained major cemeteries from Meroitic, X-Group, as well as some from Christian times) contained a number of cache pits alone or in small groups (some pits and shallow depressions were associated with the late cemetery). One cache, Q 631, contained five inverted jars, four of them rippled jars of the highest quality; they were some of the finest found by the expedition.

Since many tombs in Cemetery W were not plundered, they contained a more complete representation of the variety and quantity of goods originally deposited, and a number of tombs in both Cemeteries W and V belonged to persons of greater than average wealth. However, the structures and contents of these tombs were much less imposing than those of Cemetery L, a fact that underscores Cemetery L's uniqueness and importance.

A. CHRONOLOGY

A number of tombs in Cemetery W and some caches in Cemetery Q were dated to Middle A-Group. In fact, based on the appearance of rippled pottery and the relative lack of late painted vessels and related pottery types, more tombs in Cemetery W were assigned to the Middle than to the Late A-Group phase.[1] Cemetery V contained tombs of Late A-Group; Middle A-Group materials may have been present but could not be identified because the tombs were badly destroyed; some had later been reused. As mentioned above, Cemetery S contained four pits dating to the Late A-Group. Middle A-Group burials were found in Cemetery T but none from the Late A-Group period. The two caches with pottery in Cemetery Q were also of Middle A-Group date.

B. TOMB TYPES

Apart from cattle sacrifices and the great royal-type tomb, all of the major A-Group tomb classes were present. The most important tomb was V 59, of the quasi-royal type.[2] It had a trench about 5 m long, probably with a step and a chamber on the side. The tomb was not excavated to the chamber, though the size and shape of the trench, as well as the large number of stones it contained, indicated it was of the trench-chamber type which the expedition discovered in Cemetery L the following year. The most elaborate "patrician" tomb type, V 67, also had this plan but on a smaller scale and it was blocked with stones.

The most interesting of these tombs was an oblong trench with four holes in the bottom, a feature later found in bed burials.[3] Two A-Group examples were found at Qustul, one with a sloped ramp for access (W 11), the other a simple trench (V 61). The arrangement of four holes, one at each corner, intended either to receive a bed or to accommodate a ritual involving a bed, is one of the most important recurring features of burial archaeology in Nubia. V 59 and V 61 had apparently been altered and had walls built across the trenches to divide them. In addition, six patrician tombs had rectangular shafts, and seven were made in the usual shape, rectangular with rounded ends.

Ordinary, or "plebeian," tombs were comparatively elaborate at Qustul. Three consisted of circular pits with oval chambers (W 12, W 14, and W 20); they may have been altered cache pits. Two were simply oval, but the majority had parallel sides and rounded ends. A few common burials were made in circular pits. Some of these circular pits had evidently been made for storage but were reused.[4] Circular pits have been found in almost all A-Group cemeteries, including L, W, S, and T, although they were sometimes difficult to date. As noted above, three pits in Q contained pottery or other evidence, such as a depression in the center, which indicated their date. Although many circular pits and depressions were contemporary with the much later X-Group cemetery, a number of the empty pits could be assigned to A-Group because their placement and shape differ from the shallow depressions found near the X-Group cult structures.[5] Four common types of deposit pits were found in Qustul and Adindan, including simple circular pits with vertical sides, circular pits with depressions in the center, oval pits, and pits which were wider at the bottom than at the top.[6]

In addition to the round cache pits, a small cluster of four shafts, three of which were rectangular, were found near the south end of Cemetery S. They contained pottery and objects comparable to those in Cemetery L, with no evidence of burials. One, S 3, contained a carved sandstone slab with a rounded top which may have been part of a stela. Pits of this type were used in Cemetery L for animal sacrifices but were not generally used in

A-Group Nubia for burials or ordinary cache pits. The connection of these shafts with Cemetery L will be discussed in the conclusion of this chapter. The possibility that they have a wider significance in the development of royal funerary complexes is discussed in the concluding chapter of the volume.

C. POTTERY

Like most other A-Group sites, most of the burials at Qustul belonged to the Middle and Late A-Group, and the pottery these burials contained included most of the classes and shapes found elsewhere. With its vast quantities of painted pottery and even Syro-Palestinian type jugs, Cemetery L differed far more from other A-Group sites than did the other cemeteries at Qustul. However, the tombs considered in this volume also contained an unusual variety and number of vessels, as illustrated by a summary comparison of the relative quantities and diversity of pottery in A-Group sites given in table 4 below.

Table 4 — The Relative Quantity and Diversity of A-Group Pottery Classes

Designation		Nubia Generally		Cemetery L		Cemeteries W, V, S, T, Q	
		Amt.	Var.	Amt.	Var.	Amt.	Var.
I.	Ext. Ptd.	*-**	*-**	1k+	172+	***	**
II.	Rippled	***	**	++	++	**	**
III.	Band Inc.	*	++	—	—	—	—
IV.	Ptd.-Inc.	++	++	**	**	++	++
V.	Int. Ptd.	—+	—+	***	**	++	++
VI.	*alpha*	?	?	***	*	**	**
VI.	*beta*	—	—	***	+	*	++
VI.	*gamma*	***	**	**	*	***	**
VII.	Sud.	*-**	++-*	***	**	*?	++-*
VIII.	Hv. Inc.	-+	-+	***	**	+	+[a]
IX.	Geo. Inc.	++-*	+-++	—	—	—	—
X.	Hard Pk.	***	**	150	***	***	**
XI.	Eg. Cs.	++-*	++-*	***	*	*	++
XII.	Syr.-Pl.	—	—	*	+	—	—[b]

Key:

+	=	single	++	=	2-5
*	=	5-10	**	=	10-20
***	=	20-50	****	=	50+

150 = over 100, approximate number given

[a]rare occurrences in Sudanese Nubia

[b]only one type recognized

As noted in the table, no examples of Syro-Palestinian (type) Early Bronze I pottery were found in non-royal graves at Qustul. On the other hand, categories of material occurring elsewhere in Nubia, such as Form Groups III and IX, both related styles of incised bowls, are absent from Qustul entirely. Rippled vessels (II) are more common than they are in Cemetery L. Exterior Painted bowls (I) remain more common in the groups considered here than elsewhere in Nubia. Because these groups span a longer period than those in Cemetery L, certain classes of vessels are more diverse, especially Form Groups II (Rippled) and VI *gamma* (Simple Coarse). Because the graves in Cemetery W were not subjected to the plundering and burning that occurred in Cemetery L, the shapes and surfaces of many vessels were relatively well preserved.

The pottery presented in this volume is classified according to principles discussed in some detail in *OINE* III. A number of the Form Groups that were poorly represented in Cemetery L are subdivided in greater detail here. These divisions are based on a reconstruction of the shaping process (also discussed in *OINE* III).[7] According to that reconstruction, A-Group pottery was shaped by pressing or beating the clay against the ground in a series of distinct steps to produce each of the shapes. The classifications are based on the number of steps or stages in the process and the kind of contour produced during each step or stage.

a. A-GROUP AND OTHER LOCAL POTTERY

A-GROUP POTTERY WITH ELABORATE FINISH

Form Group I: Exterior Painted Pottery (pls. 14-17)

Over seventy-five complete and fragmentary vessels of exterior painted pottery were found in cemeteries other than Cemetery L. They were almost all large conical bowls (A), although a few small bowls (B, E), cups (C), and pinched oval boats (D) were also found. Only one unusual shape type could be assigned to this group (F) (table 5). Decoration on the bowls consisted of the linear-geometric and overall painted designs with some combinations. One representational painted vessel was found in Cemetery S, a tall, overhemispherical cup with bird figures and a band of triangles with hatching in opposite directions. Except for this example, the exterior painted bowls occurred here in much the same way they occurred elsewhere in Lower Nubia.

Numbered and ordered as in *OINE* III,[8] the following classification is presented according to the decorative element or motif; the code for the shape, an uppercase letter, follows in parentheses (see table 6 below).

For the colors of Form Group I, see tomb register entries W 10—1; W 19—4, 11, 12; W 27—1; and V 67—16 and 24.[9]

Table 5—Shapes of Form Group I, Exterior Painted Pottery

A. Tall, deep, convex tapered bowls with narrow flattened bases	fig. 3f
B. Wide, deep (more shallow than A) bowls with a vertical or sharply curved upper side which tapers to a narrow, flattened or (rarely) pointed base.	fig. 3a, e
C. Tall, convex, nearly cylindrical cups, almost always with flattened bases.	fig. 4j
D. Boat-shaped vessels with pinched sides. (Only one painted vessel of this shape was found in cemeteries other than L.)	fig. 49f
E. Shallow convex bowls. (Few vessels of this shape were found in cemeteries other than L.)	fig. 51d
F. Unusual Shapes	fig. 5c

Table 6—Register of Form Group I, Exterior Painted Pottery

Key

2.

W 19   motif

    tomb

3   vessel as numbered object in tomb (if omitted, the vessel is a sherd)

A   vessel as it occurs in the category (if the letter occurs alone, the vessel is a sherd)

(B)   shape code

2. Simple opposed-hatching:
   W 19 11—B (B)

4. Opposed-hatching in contiguous bands or pairs of bands (fig. 3a):
   W 10—12 E (B, clusters of 3); W 10—3 C (A, long, impaled); W 19—4 (B); S 2 A (A)

5. Simple crosshatched bands or areas (fig. 3b):
   V 65 C

6. Horizontal lines or bands filled with horizontal lines (fig. 3e):
   W 19—12 C (B); W 11—6 C (A)

7. Hatched triangles, pendant (fig. 3f):
   W 10—2 B (A)

9. Hatched triangles, opposed tip to tip (fig. 3c):
   V 59 D (A)

10. Opposed-hatched triangles in the same band, side to side (fig. 3d):
    V 67—24 E (A), V 65 B (A); S 2 B (A), C (A?)

23. Opposed-nested triangles or cut-off zigzags or lozenges (fig. 3g-h):
    S 2 D (A?), E (A?); S 3 D (A?), E (A?)

27. Solid triangles (fig. 3j):
    V 59 E (C); S 2 F (A)

32. Opposed-hatched rectangles in the same band; the rectangular weave pattern (fig. 3i):
    W 10—4 D (B); W 19—15 D (B); W 11—4 A (A); V 65 A (B); V 67—24 (C)

34. Solid rectangles (fig. 3k):
    V 61 D

38. Long, feathered strokes, aligned (fig. 4a):
    W 2—1 A (A, 38-39); V 59—1 A (A, 38-39), B; V 61 E (C, 38-39); V 67 H (A); K (38-45); S 3 B (A), C (C)

39. Same, alternated (fig. 4e; see entry 38):
    S 4 A; V 59 A (A, 38-39), H (A)

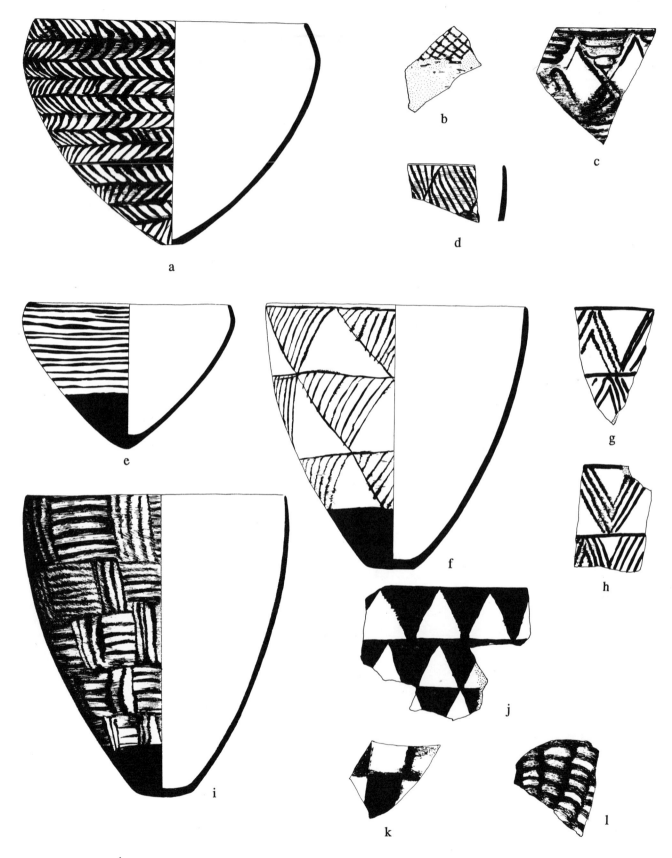

Figure 3. Painted designs of Form Group I, Exterior Painted pottery: (a) 4, W 19—4; (b) 5, V 65, C; (c) 9,
V 59, D; (d) 10, V 65, B; (e) 6, W 19—12; (f) 7, W 10—2; (g-h) 23, S 2, D; (i) 10, V 67—24; (j) 27,
S 2, F; (k) 34, V 61, D; (l) 41, V 59, G. Scale 2:5.

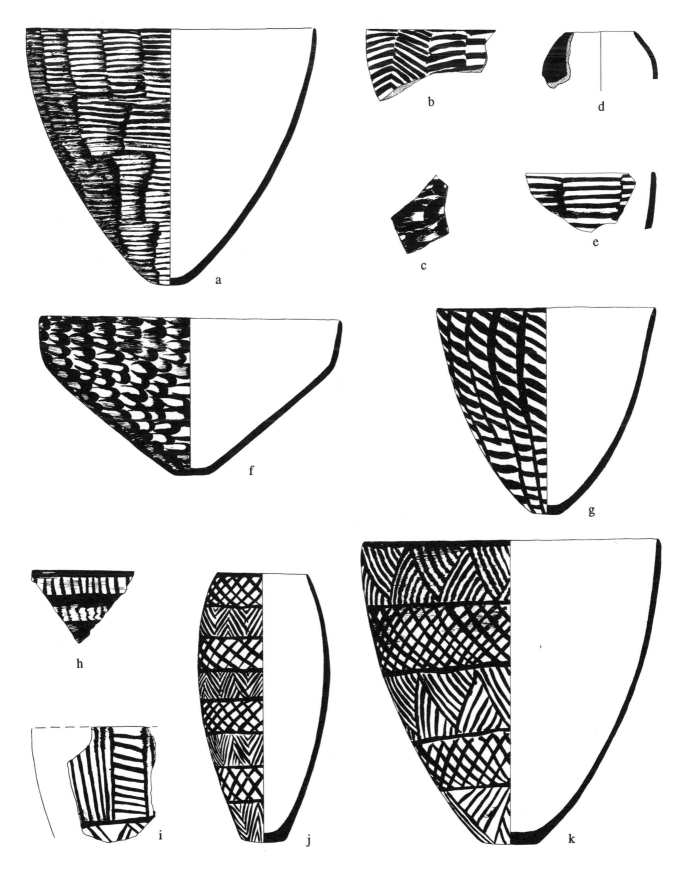

Figure 4. Painted designs of Form Group I, Exterior Painted pottery: (a) 38-39, W 2—1; (b) 46, V 61, A; (c) 47, V 61, B; (d) 50, V 61, F; (e) 39, S 4, A; (f) 48, V 67—22; (g) 55, V 67—13; (h) 58, V 65, I; (i) 121, V 67—16; (j) 81b, S 3, A; (k) 82, W 11—5. Scale 2:5.

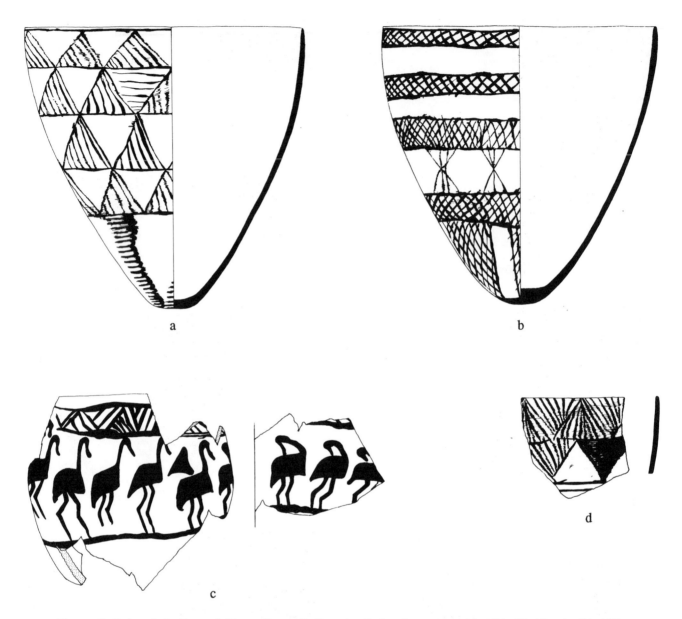

Figure 5. Painted designs of Form Group I, Exterior Painted pottery: (a) 174, W 10—1; (b) 173, W 10—13; (c) 176, S 3—9; (d) 175, V 65, D. Scale 2:5.

Table 6—Register of Form Group I, Exterior Painted Pottery — Cont.

40. Short strokes, aligned (see entry 38):
    V 67 I (A, 40-41)
41. Same, alternated (fig. 3l; see entry 38):
    V 61 C (A); V 59 G
42. Vertical strokes (see entry 38)

Table 6—Register of Form Group I, Exterior Painted Pottery — Cont.

44. Vertical arched strokes in alternating directions:
V 59 C? (B? below an uncertain motif)

45. Strokes at an angle, painted vertically, the tail of the stroke above leading to the head of the stroke below (see entry 38)

46. Herringbone, strokes alternated (fig. 4b):
W 11—10 D (A, vertical); V 59 F (D, probably aligned); V 61 A (A); V 67—15 B (A)

47. Joined, double strokes feathered in the center, large (fig 4c):
V 61 B; V 67—25 F (A)

48. Same, small (fig. 4f):
V 67—22 D (B)

49. Blobs, alternated:
V 67 J

50. Solid (fig. 4d):
V 65 G (C), V 67 L (C), V 61 F (C)

55. Vertical, hatching or opposed-hatching in bands; equivalent of 55 in *OINE* III, which is a combination (fig. 4g):
V 67—13 A (A)

57. Combinations of opposed-hatching in contiguous bands and crosshatching:
V 65 F

58. Crosshatching (also includes vertical hatching or lines) or opposed-hatching in contiguous bands and horizontal bands (fig. 4h):
V 65 I (A), J (A)

81b. Opposed triangles above vertical opposed-hatching in bands (fig 4j):
S 3 A (A)

82. Opposed triangles with crosshatched bands (fig. 4k):
W 11—5 B (A); V 65 E (E) 121. Nested triangles (with impaled centers), crosshatched bands (fig. 4i):
V 67—16 C (C)

141/142. Opposed-hatched rectangles above medium, aligned, or alternated strokes:
V 67—26 G (B); V 67—24 E (A)

173. Crosshatched bands above vertical crosshatched panels, one band of rosettes or asterisks (fig. 5b):
W 10—13 F (A)

174. Standing hatched triangles above separated, vertical bands of strokes (fig 5a):
W 10—1 A (A)

175. a. Opposed triangles above, hatched below, filled in with lines spreading from the apex. b. Pendant triangles with hatching and solid paint. c. Horizontal lines (fig. 5d):
V 65 D (A)

176. Band of opposed-hatched triangles above separated band of birds, some with necks reversed, and triangle (fig. 5c):
S 3—9 F (F)

Uncertain, possibly combination of 32 and 119: S 2 G

Form Group II: Rippled Pottery (pls. 19-20)

Because some tombs were earlier than the main period of Cemetery L, the ripple-burnished pottery characteristic of Middle A-Group is substantially more important in Cemeteries W and Q.[10] This Form Group also has a wider range of shapes than the exterior painted vessels, although special shapes, such as cups, boats, and fancy forms, occur less frequently (table 7). The rippled pottery here includes many vessels comparable with those found nearby, in northern Sudan, but they are much less numerous and less diverse; for example, tall cups are found among the rippled vessels in Sudan.[11] Also, as in Sudan, most of the vessels have milled rims. The following classification is based on the stages that can be distinguished in the shaping of the vessel.

For the colors of Form Group II, see the tomb register entries W 8—2, W 11—9 and 15.

Table 7—Register of Form Group II, Rippled Pottery

A.   Conical bowl (1 stage, side; fig. 6a):
   1.   wide:
        W 15—5 B
   2.   narrow:
        see *OINE* X[a]

B.   Conical bowl with flattened base (2 stages, side and base; fig. 6b):
   1.   narrow base:
        W 11—14 C
   2.   broader base:
        see *OINE* X

C.   Bowl with a conical lower side and an abrupt curve or bend to the upper side (2 stages, lower side and upper side; fig. 6c):
   1.   curved base:
        W 8—2 A; W 21—1
   2.   flattened base:
        see *OINE* X
   3.   broad base:
        see *OINE* X

D.   Convex cup or beaker with a pointed base (3 stages, lower side, upper side, point base; fig. 6d):
        W 11—9 A

E.   Broad bowl with flat or slightly convex base, angled side (2 stages, base, side; fig. 6e):
        W 15—4 A, W 23—3 A

F.   Bowl with flat or slightly convex base, vertical or inverted side (2 stages, base, side; fig. 6f):
        W 11—15 B

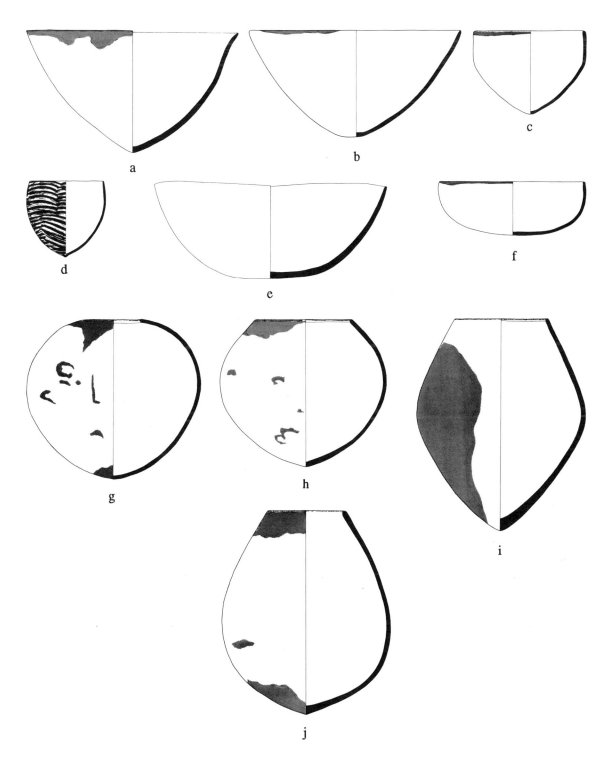

Figure 6. Shapes of Form Group II, Rippled pottery: (a) A, W 15—5; (b) B, W 11—14; (c) C, W 21—1; (d) D, W 11—9; (e) E, W 15—4; (f) F, W 11—15; (g) G, Q 631—1; (h) H, Q 631—2; (i) I, Q 631—3; (j) J, Q 631—4. Scale 1:5.

Table 7—Register of Form Group II, Rippled Pottery — Cont.

G.   Globular jar (2 stages; bottom, side; fig. 6g):
   1.   broad, with hole-mouth:
        Q 631—1 A
   2.   open:
        see *OINE* X

H.   Curved, almost biconical jar (3 stages, lower side, curved waist, upper side; fig. 6h):
        Q 631—2 B

I.   Biconical jar with nearly carinated waist (2 stages, lower side, upper side; fig. 6i):
        Q 631—3 C

J.   Bag-shaped jar with pointed base (3 stages, conical base, curved waist, long upper side; fig. 6j):
        Q 631—4 D

---

[a]References to *OINE* X indicate vessels found in A-Group tombs in Cemetery B at Serra East which do not occur at Qustul.

Form Group III: Band-Incised Pottery

No pottery of this group was found in the present material.

Form Group IV: Painted and Incised-Impressed Pottery

Sherds from three painted and incised-impressed vessels were found in V 59 and V 61. Broad, red diagonal and horizontal bands frame diagonal parallelogram-shaped zones, sometimes framed by incised lines and/or filled in by rolled rectangular impressions.[12] The vessels were the same shape as A in Form Group I.

Form Group V: Interior Painted Bowls (pl. 33)

Sherds of two interior painted bowls were found in V 65. The first had the same open, curved shape and flattened rim found in Cemetery L and was decorated with poorly painted perpendicular lines extending from the rim. The exterior and a band about 2 cm wide inside the vessel had been red washed, and it had fire blooms or smudges. The second sherd was painted with crude, horizontal strokes. One other vessel, W 6—14, had a broad band of red applied around the inside of the rim. The vessel is classified here as coarse (VI *gamma*), and it illustrates a transitional combination of features occurring in the Middle A-Group period which led to the development of interior painted bowls.[13]

By far, the most interesting vessel of this group is a local imitation of an Egyptian hard pink bowl (X-G), W 11—8. However, it was shaped by local methods from clay containing remains of chaff and was not as highly fired as comparable Egyptian vessels. The surface is light orange or red-yellow, and it has been completely burnished, whereas contemporary Egyptian potters burnished a horizontal band below the rim on the outside and made an open pattern of vertical streaks on the inside of the vessels. The bowl was decorated with designs painted in red on both the interior and exterior. Inside the bowl are lines that spiral from the center to the rim. Outside are four groups of angled lines that form large triangles extending point downward from the rim; these triangles have vertical lines extending from the apex to the center of the vessel's base. This design is comparable to that on an interior painted bowl from L 17, which has solid triangles with pendant lines on the exterior and groups of vertical zigzag lines on the interior. The decoration on this bowl is also closely related to that on an Egyptian jar from W 6 and Egyptian bowls from L 23 and L 19; it is discussed in detail in another work.[14]

For the colors of Form Group V, see tomb register entry W 11—8.

A-GROUP ORDINARY POTTERY

Form Group VI alpha: *Simple Fine Pottery* (pls. 21, 22a-c, 23a-c, g-h)

Because the contents of a number of tombs in Cemetery L had been burned, it was often difficult to characterize the original surfaces of unpainted vessels. In Cemetery W, a number of fine, unpainted vessels were found either undamaged or broken but complete, thus permitting the vessels to be described with greater confidence. The clay and temper are essentially the same as those used to make the exterior painted bowls, but most shapes are different (table 8). The V-shaped bowl with a narrow, flattened base appears in this group, but there are also a number of convex bowls, tapered cups, and wide bowls with broad, flat bases. The fine, undecorated pottery includes shapes that appear in the other A-Group categories. Some vessels were coated red, and most of the surfaces were smoothed or lightly burnished. This burnish, generally less complete than that on painted vessels, was made with horizontal strokes near the rim, inside and out, and vertical strokes across the interior and sometimes the exterior as well. The vessel was fired pink-drab inside and mottled with fire blooms and smudges on the outside, as is typical of A-Group pottery. As with the rippled pottery, the classification is based on the stages that can be distinguished in the shaping of the vessel.[15]

The shapes of this Form Group were not classified in *OINE* III; most of the vessels published in that volume could be classified in E of this Form Group.

For the colors of Form Group VI *alpha*, see tomb register entries, W 6—12, W 10—11, and W 32—4.

Table 8—Register of Form Group VI *alpha*, Simple Fine Pottery

A. Convex, conical bowl (1 stage, side; fig 7c):
    W 10—14 B; W 32—4 B

B. Conical bowl with flattened base (2 stages, side and bottom, same as Form Group I A):
    1. narrow base (fig. 7e):
        W 32—3 A
    2. broad base (fig. 7f):
        V 67—14 B

C. Bowl with conical lower side, bend or curve to upper side (2 stages, lower side and upper side, same as Form Group I B):
    1. convex upper side (fig. 7d):
        W 10—11 A
    2. upper side curved inward (fig. 7g):
        W 25—1 A; V 65 A(?)

D. Deep bowl with a convex base and side (2 stages, base, side; fig 7h):
    W 23—2 A; W 27—1 A

E. Open and small bowls:
    1. Open convex bowls (1 stage, single curve):
        a   wide (fig. 7a):
        W 6—12 A, 13 B; W 19—14 C; V 59 A
        b. narrow (fig. 7b):
        W 9—2 A (hor. burnish); V 52—1 A (red)
    2. Cup with curved base, curved side (2 stages, base, side; fig. 7i):
        W 15—2 A
    3. Flat base, straight side (2 stages, base, side):
        a   narrow base, tall side (fig. 7j):
        W 2—2 A; W 11—12 A
        b. equal base and side:
        W 19—5 A, V 67—12 A (red)
        c. broad base, short, angled side (fig. 7k):
        W 19—10 B

F. Boat (stages uncertain; fig. 7l):
    W 2—5 B

G. Unusual shapes:
    1. strainer with small holes (fig. 20c):
        W 7—6 C

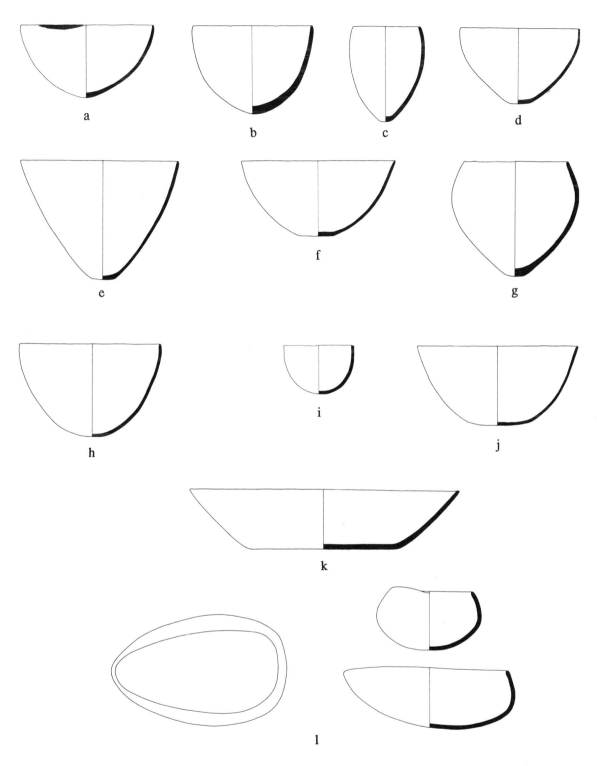

Figure 7. Shapes of Form Group VI *alpha*, Fine Simple pottery: (a) E1a, W 6—12; (b) E1b, V 52—1; (c) A, W 10—14; (d) C1, W 10—11; (e) B1, W 32—3; (f) B2, V 67—14; (g) C2, W 25—1; (h) D, W 23—2; (i) E2, W 15—2; (j) E3a, W 2—2; (k) E3c, W 19—10; (l) F, W 2—5. Scale 1:5.

Form Group VI beta: *Miniature Cups* (pl. 22 d-i)

Miniature cups or jars were less common than they were in Cemetery L (table 9). Two of the pieces from W 10 have red coats and were burnished vertically; one has fire blooms and smudges. Three shapes are recognized here: the usual bag-shape (A), a bag-shaped jar with a flat base (B), and a single squat jar with a narrow neck (C).[16]

For the colors of Form Group VI *beta*, see tomb register entries W 7—3, W 8—3, and V 67—10.

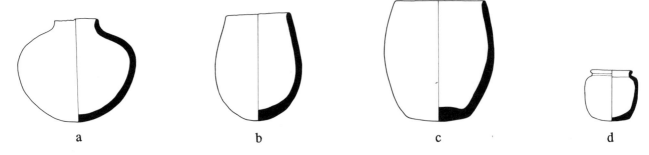

a   b   c   d

Figure 8. Shapes of Form Group VI *beta*, Miniature cups: (a) C, W 7—3; (b) A, W 11—24; (c) B, W 8—3; (d) C, S 3—3, A or C. Scale 2:5.

Table 9—Register of Form Group VI *beta*, Miniature Cups

Shape	Vessel	Remarks and Illustration
C	W 7—3	(fig. 8a)
B	W 8—3	(fig. 8c)
A	W 10—21	Red coat and burnish
A	W 10—23A	Red coat and burnish
A	W 11—24	(fig. 8b)
A?	W 19—3	
A	S 3—1	
A	S 3—2	
A or C	S 3—3	(fig. 8d)
A	V 61 A	
A?	V 67—10A	
A?	V 67—11	

Form Group VI gamma: *Simple Coarse Pottery* (pls. 23d-f, 24-25)

The category of locally made, coarse vessels makes up a much greater proportion of the material than it did in Cemetery L. It was also substantially more varied, due, at least partly, to the date. Most of the vessels in this group are jars, closed containers which disappeared almost completely from local pottery by the Late A-Group period (table 10). Almost all the jars presented here belonged to the Middle A-Group, before local containers were completely replaced by Egyptian jars.

The clay used for these vessels appears to have been the same as that used for other A-Group pottery. Mineral particles of various sizes; irregular, limy particles; and irregular voids, where pieces of chaff had burned away, indicate that the clay contained some kind of earth or soil and a little straw.

The shapes include almost all the vessel shapes and sizes which occur in this period. The smallest are cups, and there are some vessels whose shapes resemble interior painted bowls. The next size is an almost globular jar about 25 cm high. Slightly larger, and more important, is a jar about 25 to 35 cm high with a curved upper and tapered lower side and a flattened or stump base. A very low vertical neck or rim is the only elaboration found in the shapes of these vessels.

Normally, the coarse surface was just wiped or scraped horizontally, a process which often left a swag pattern around the exterior of the vessel.[17] As with other ordinary vessels, the jars were not usually burnished, and they were rarely given a red coat. Firing was much the same as in other groups, but fire blooms and smudges are less prominent. The atmosphere may have been more steadily neutral or oxidizing, at least toward the end of the firing. Once again, this classification is based on the stages that can be detected in the shaping of the vessel.[18]

For colors of Form Group VI *gamma*, see tomb register entries W 15—1 and W 23—4.

Table 10—Form Group VI *gamma*, Simple Coarse Pottery

A.   Convex bowl and cups (1 stage, curved vessel):
  1.   open (fig. 9a):
    W 6—14 B
  2.   small cup (fig. 9b):
    W 6—16 C

B.   Narrow, conical cup (1 stage, side; fig. 9c):
    W 32—5 A

C.   Jar with upper side curved inward (2 stages, curved base, curved side; fig. 9d):
    W 7—2 B

D.   Vessel with conical lower body, curved upper side (2 stages, cone, curve; fig. 9e):
    W 7—1 A

E.   Bowl with curved base, angled side (2 stages, base, side; fig 9f):
    W 6—15 B

F.   Jar with convex base and side (3 stages, all curves; fig. 9g):
    W 16—1 A (everted neck); Q 80—1 A

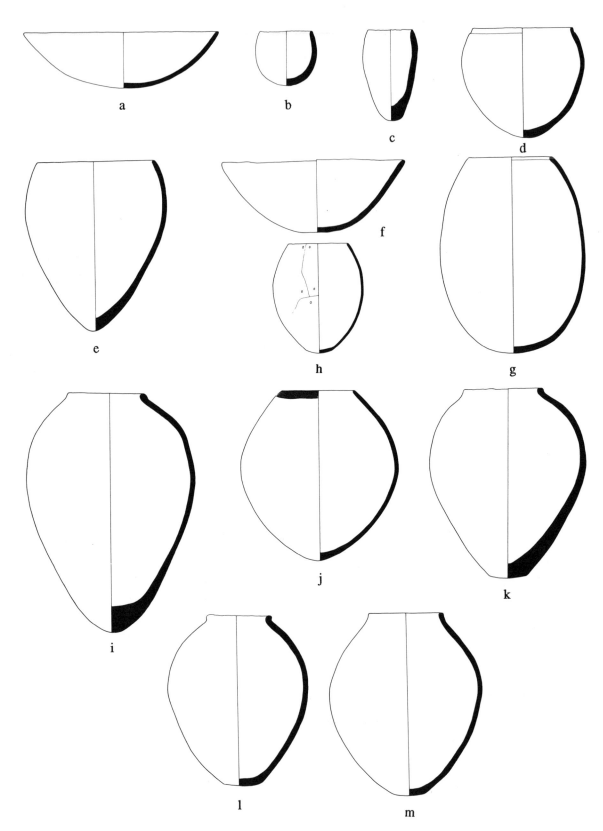

Figure 9. Shapes of Form Group VI *gamma*, Simple Coarse pottery: (a) A1, W 6—14; (b) A2, W 6—16; (c) B, W 32—5; (d) C, W 7—2; (e) D, W 7—1; (f) E, W 6—15; (g) F, Q 80—1; (h) G, W 5—2; (i) H, W 8—1; (j) I, W 15—1; (k) J, W 33—1; (l) K, W 23—4; (m) L, W 11—21. Scale 1:5.

Table 10—Form Group VI *gamma*, Simple Coarse Pottery — Cont.

G. Jar with curved base, open, curved side (2 stages, curved base, open curve; fig 9h):
W 5—2 A

H. Jar with conical lower side, curve to upper side, everted or rib rim (3 stages, cone, curve, everted neck; fig. 9i):
W 8—1 A; W 26—1 A

I. Jar with biconical or bicurved side (2 stages, equal cones or curves; fig 9j):
W 15—1 A

J. Jar with flattened base, conical lower side, curved upper side (3 stages with rim, as described; fig. 9k):
W 33—1 A; W 23—1 A

K. Jar with flattened base, bicurved side (3 stages and rim, base, lower side, upper side; fig 9l):
W 11—3 A; W 6—6 A; W 23—4 B; W 23—7 C; W 5—3 B

L. Jar, same as K, neck (four stages, same as K, with neck; fig. 9m):
W 11—21 B

M. Very large bowl, coffin?
OINE X[a]

[a]The reference to *OINE* X indicates a vessel found in an A-Group tomb in Cemetery B at Serra East which does not occur at Qustul.

Form Group VII: Sudanese Overall Zone-Incised Pottery

Only one complete vessel made in the Sudanese tradition was found in Cemetery W (W 38—2). It was a tall bowl or cup with a conical lower- and curved upper- body. The cup has a band of vertical zigzags above the waist and rocker patterns below it, decoration typical of the Sudanese tradition; it had also been smudged in a fire. A second vessel, with the same shape and vertical zigzag decoration, was found among the sherds from V 59 (A-1).[19]

For the colors of this Form Group, see the tomb register entry V 59 VII A.

Form Group VIII: Heavy Incised Bowl

One heavy incised bowl was found in V 67 (23, dec. class 12; pls. 34, 35). The bowl is convex and much deeper than the squat bowls from Cemetery L. The rim is sharply bent inward, making a wide, flat surface. This surface was decorated with a wavy band in reserve, perhaps a modification of the serpent common on such vessels. A series of wavy bands extend across the bottom of the bowl; empty bands alternate with bands containing rows of puncture marks. These rows tend to be organized into vaguely geometric shapes, especially rectangular shapes. Two small areas within the filled zones contain animals formed by groups of puncture marks: a bovine (?) and a bird. Although plans, or landscapes, are customarily considered a much later invention in representational art, the animals on this bowl seem almost to suggest that a landscape-setting of some kind was intended. In a very general way, it is reminiscent of the lower part of the Scorpion macehead. The effect is enhanced by the rectangular areas filled in with puncture marks.[20] The bowl was fired grey-buff to black.

For the colors of this Form Group, see tomb register entry V 67—23.

Form Group IX

No pottery of this kind was found at Qustul.

b. EGYPTIAN POTTERY

Form Group X: Egyptian Hard Pink Pottery (pls. 26-32a)

Egyptian hard pink pottery made up most of the jars or closed containers found in the concession (table 11). However, there were fewer Egyptian bowls than were found in Cemetery L and none of the largest storage jars; most containers from these cemeteries are smaller narrow and ovoid storage jars (shapes W and X). Of special interest is an ovoid storage jar with three lug handles on the shoulder and painted decoration (X1b). The significance of this painted jar is discussed below.[21] The following classification corresponds to the one given in *OINE* III.

For the colors of Form Group X, see tomb register entries for W 6—4, 5; W 10—1, 6, 7, 19; W 11—13; W 22—1; and W 32—1.

Table 11—Register of Form Group X, Egyptian Hard Pink Pottery

---

BOWLS

C.   Convex, with high side (fig. 10a):
    W 10—6 B, 9 E

E.   Open, with convex upper side and taper to base (fig. 10b):
    W 10—10 F, 17 G (very irregular shape), 20 I; V 59 A(?)

F.   Same, medium height (fig. 10c):
    W 6—8 E (unburnished), W 31—1 A, V 67—2 A (deformed oval); T 128—3 A

G.   Same, tall (fig. 10d):
    W 11—13 C (very large, unburnished)

L.   Evenly or slightly curved, with bent-out rim, tall:
    W 19—16

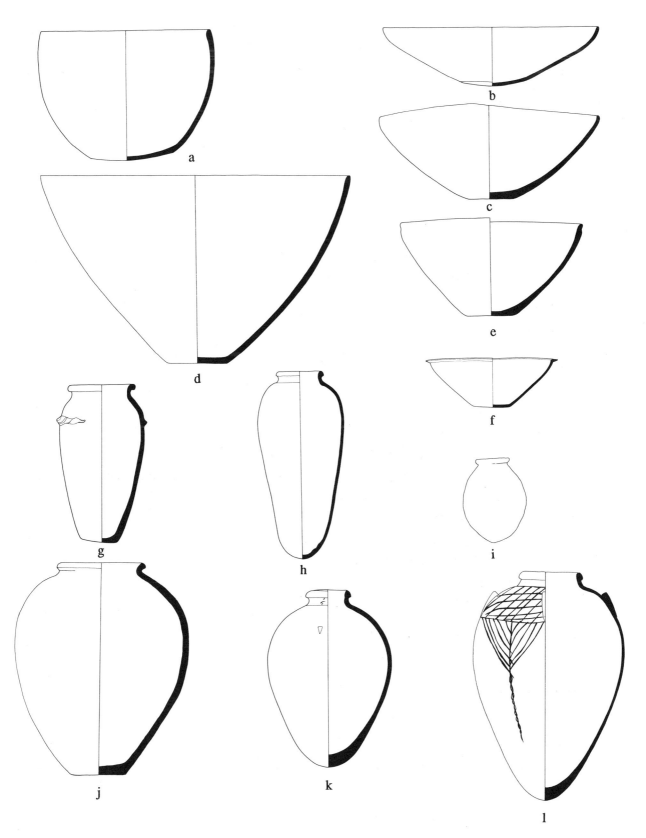

Figure 10. Shapes of Form Group X, Egyptian Hard Pink pottery: (a) C, W 10—6; (b) E, W 10—20; (c) F, W 6—8; (d) G, W 11—13; (e) M1, W 6—7; (f) M2, V 67—21; (g) P, W 22—1; (h) W, W 6—2; (i) R2, T 110—2; (j) AB, T 75—1; (k) X1a, W 10—7; (l) X1b, W 6—5. Scale 1:5 except (h), (k), (l) 1:10.

Table 11—Register of Form Group X, Egyptian Hard Pink Pottery — Cont.

M.   Side bent in toward top (to vertical):
     1. With bead rim (fig. 10e):
              W 6—7 D (unburnished)
     2. With bent-out rim (fig. 10f):
              W 10—19 H, V 67—21 B

JARS

P.   Wavy-handled jars (includes cylinder jars in *OINE* III fig. 10g):
          W 22—1 A; T 113—1 A

R2. Globular flask (fig. 10i):
          T 110—2 B

W.   Narrow, tapered jar with short neck and roll-rim (fig 10h):
          W 5—1 A; W 6—2 A; W 10—8 D, W 32—1 A, 2 B; Q 80—2 A, 16 ?; T 110—1 A

X.   Ovoid storage jar with neck and rim as W:
     1. Sloping shoulder:
          a No special features (fig 10k):
              W 10—5 A (elaborate potmark), 7 C (potmark); W 11—2 B (potmark: granary and meander
              superimposed), 1 A (potmark: simple animal);
              W 6—4 B (narrow neck)
          b. Three lugs (fig. 10l):
              W 6—5 C (painting as described)
     2. Horizontal shoulder:
              W 19—2 A

AA. Lentoid jar (fig. 52n):
     V 65—A

AB. Tapered jar with flat base, everted rim (fig. 10j):
     T 75—1 A

Unc. Bowl. V 59 A

Form Group XI: Egyptian Coarse Pottery (pl. 32b)

A few pieces of Egyptian coarse pottery were found in Cemeteries W and T (table 12). Sherds of two pierced, polygonal stands were found, which were probably tall like their counterparts in Cemetery L. Otherwise, coarse vessels included only the beer jar with a pierced strainer and a conical jar.[22]

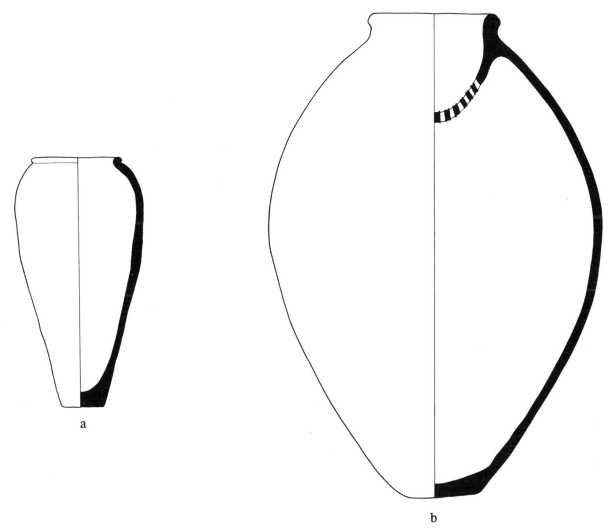

Figure 11. Shapes of Form Group XI, Egyptian Coarse pottery: (a) B, T 128—1; (b) A, W 6—3. Scale (a) 1:5, (b) 2:5.

Table 12—Register of Form Group XI, Egyptian Coarse Pottery

A. Strainer jars (fig. 11b): W 6—3 A; W 19—1 A

B. Conical jar with flattened or stump base (fig. 11a): T 113—2 A, 3 B; T 128—1 A, possibly B

C. Stands (fig. 19): Surface finds SW of W 6, both from large, polygonal stands: A, B

D. OBJECTS

Like the pottery, objects other than metal tools and weapons were fewer and of lower quality than their counterparts in Cemetery L. However, they tended to be richer than most found elsewhere in A-Group.[23] Many categories of objects that were found in Cemetery L were also present: incense burners, mortars, pestles, palettes, jewelry, pigments, among others. Some, such as shell hooks and related shell objects, which make up a large a part of the material recovered from Cemetery L, were missing. The most remarkable luxury items were the incense and ivory objects.

a. A-GROUP OBJECTS

INCENSE BURNERS

Two incense burners were found in these groups, both of the low type with an oval profile and a concave depression in the upper surface. One, from W 19 (6), is made of sandstone, and the other, from S 4 (1), is composed of a clay mixture. These incense burners have the simplest shape found in A-Group and are undecorated.[24]

MORTARS AND PESTLES (pl. 36e)

Four mortars, two with their pestles, were found in Cemeteries W, V, and S. Two belong to the class of irregular, oval mortars (A), one of banded brown quartzite (S 2—1) and the other of simple brown quartzite (V 67—19). The third, W 19—7, is of grey quartz with colored bands. Both mortars W 19—7 and V 67—18 have the shape commonly seen in Cemetery L: sharp curves which form four corners and evenly curved sides and ends.[25] The two pestles that accompanied the mortars from V 67 (19) and W 19 (7) are oblong, oval objects made of quartz; the one from V 67 is grey. Two other pestles of the same shape but without mortars were found in Q 80 (3-4). The pestles were worn on the sides so that their cross-sections are no longer round but oval.

PALETTES (pls. 38, 39)

Eighteen palettes were found in Cemetery W, two in S and three in V 67 (table 13). In addition, two crude stone objects from Q 80 had apparently been used as palettes but showed no evidence of definite shaping, although their surfaces had been pecked to roughen them. The palettes mainly belong to the same classes as those found in Cemetery L, although two classes were found only in W and two (E and F) were found only in L. All of the palettes from W, S, and V are quartz; several of them are stained or have caked malachite deposits on them.[26] V 67—6 (D) has legs.

Table 13—Register of Palettes

A. Oval shape with irregular contours and varying proportions; pecked and ground (fig. 12a):
    W 2—8; W 8—4; W 7—5; W 15—3; Q 80—5, 6

B. Curve change at the ends; oval shape with fairly narrow contour, regular shape (fig. 12b):
    W 2—7

C. Curve change at four "corners"; subrectangular with straighter ends and sides (fig. 12c):
    W 5—4; W 6—11; W 11—11; W 33—2; S 3—5

D. Curve change at "corners" and the middle of the side; rhomboid (fig. 12d):
    W 2—4; W 6—9; W 10—16; W 11—20; W 19—8; W 23—6; W 38—3; S 3—4; V 67—6 (four legs), 7, 8

Not classified:
    W 9—1; W 23—8

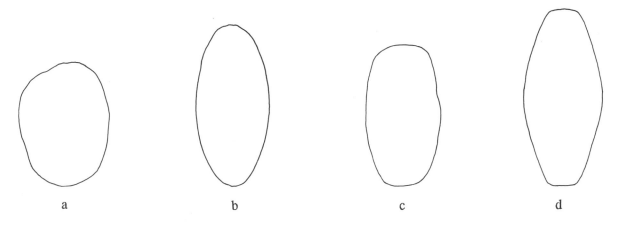

Figure 12. Shapes of palettes: (a) A, W 8—4; (b) B, W 2—7; (c) C, W 6—11; (d) D, W 10—16. Scale 2:5.

JEWELRY (pls. 41, 52)

Jewelry is not a common feature of ordinary A-Group burials. In fact, only a few beads were found in Cemeteries W and T, and their shapes were not elaborate enough to establish a classification (see pl. 37f-p).[27] Other items of jewelry included bracelets of bone and shell, some of which were decorated, a ring, a few pendants, and cowrie shells (table 14).

Table 14—Register of Jewelry

Bracelets, bone and shell:

    S 1—2 (6 simple); V 67—1 (4, dec. with incised lines)

Ring:

    S 2—3 (2)

Beads (for illustrations, see tomb register; for typology *OINE* III, pp. 120–21, and for sizes, see *OINE* V, table 40, p. 83):

    W 11—23; W 19—9; W 20—1; W 22—2; W 29—1; T 75—2; T 113—5 (n/a); T 243—1

Pendants (n/a):

    S 1—1; 3 carnelian

Cowrie shell, backs of whorls removed, aperture facing outward:

    V 67—1 and 5 (total 65)

Pebbles (pl. 44)

Pebbles were found with palettes, where they had evidently been used to grind eye paint, and also in separate deposits without palettes. In some cases, the number found was not recorded, and only a sample was retained (table 15). However, it is clear that these deposits contained more pebbles than would be required for grinding. The five pebbles in W 6—5 were found below skull A, indicating that they had probably had a religious or magical purpose.[28]

Other Local Objects and Objects or Materials of Uncertain Origin

Few other local objects were found in these groups. Q 80, a storage pit, contained three jars sealed with stones covered with dome-shaped mud seals. Among other objects, these vessels yielded three bone tools (8, 9, and 11) and fragments which were borers or awls, a cortex-backed flint blade (7) with coarse denticulate retouch and signs of wear, and a flake (12). Ostrich eggshells were found in S 1 (3) and S 4 (2), and S 3 contained three ivory objects: a pin with a decorated head (6),[29] a bag-shaped jar with suspension holes (7), and a fragment of a second jar (8).[30]

One object of special interest was assembled from a number of fragments found in V 67 (9). This was a bar or block cut from a cake of resin which had been modeled by hand. The hand-modeled surfaces have a texture that appears almost powdery, but the three cut sides have a nearly glossy appearance. The tool used to cut the

Table 15—Register of Pebbles

Tomb	Pebbles with Palettes	Pebbles as Separate Deposits
W 2	1[a] (with obj. 4)	8 (in pot 2, obj. 3)
W 6	3 (with obj. 9)	5 (under skull A, obj. 17)
W 8	1 (obj. 5)	
W 9	3 (with obj. 1)	
W 10	1 (obj. 18)	
W 11		? (obj. 22)
W 32		6 (obj. 6)
W 38	1 (with obj. 3)	
V 67		? (obj. 20)
S 2		? (obj. 2)
Q 80	1 (obj. 10)	

[a]The first digit in each entry gives the number of pebbles.

substance made an even incision and must have been made of metal. The material is the same as the reddish brown resin from Cemetery L, and similar material can be observed on a few of the incense burners from the cemetery. The substance burns with a smoky yellow flame and gives off an incense-like aroma. A great deal of ash is produced; in fact, the material expands considerably during burning, which would account for the large amounts of black deposit not only on the tops, but also on the sides of some of the incense burners which were found. The resin seems to fit the description of myrrh, but chemical analysis of it is not yet complete.

The size and shape of this cut bar suggests that it was originally part of a much larger piece. No actual cake or patty of resin was found, but oval objects of poorly fired clay mixed with straw found in W 6 (10) and L 23 could very well have been bread models or models of such cakes. Even if these cannot be identified as models of incense cakes with certainty, they have no obvious utilitarian purpose and should be regarded as models.[31]

b. EGYPTIAN OBJECTS

Apart from the ivory objects, which could be either Egyptian or local, there were very few Egyptian objects in these tombs. One alabaster cup with a flat base and a beaded rim was found in S 1 (4). A group of copper implements from W 11 (16-19) included an awl, two chisels, an axe, and a harpoon.[32] Copper awls set in bone handles were found in W 38 (4) and V 67 (4).

c. Other Materials and Samples

A number of materials were not numerous or distinctive enough to be given a detailed discussion. Their occurrence is noted in table 16 below.

Table 16—Register of Samples

Leather, "loincloth"	V 52—2
Leather, "loincloth"	V 57—1
Leather, tied	Q 80—15
Malachite	W 15—6
	Q 80—14
Ochre	W 10—22
	Q 80—13 ?
Durra seeds	W 31—2
Ostrich eggshell	S 1—3
	S 4—2

E. Artistic and Epigraphic Evidence

A seal, two painted pottery vessels, and some of the marks on the pottery parallel and complement the artistic and epigraphic evidence from Cemetery L.

IVORY CYLINDER SEAL, W 2—6

Although the surface is somewhat deteriorated, the essential structure of the design on the ivory cylinder seal from W 2 could be recovered. The object was broken in two, leaving a crack across the main figure. The decoration was framed by grooves near the top and bottom of the seal. The incised decoration consists of a stick figure of a kneeling (?) human who confronts a panel made up of vertical lines with diagonals between them. A pottery seal and a seal impression with comparable compositions in which the figure is standing were discovered in Sudanese Nubia.[33]

For the purpose of interpretation, these seals can be compared to some of the finer seals and other representations found in Nubia. The representation on the W 2 seal, though simpler, probably illustrates the same kind of event that appears on a seal from Faras[34] which shows a man who sits sprawled before a palace facade. He appears to be bleeding from the head. This same combination of a (bleeding?) man and palace facade forms the basic composition of sealings from Siali as well.[35] All of these seal compositions can be considered representations of the early sacrificial ritual, a theme most completely revealed on the Qustul Incense Burner and in the Hierakonpolis Painted Tomb.[36]

POTMARKS (fig. 13)

Potmarks which could generally be assigned to the various categories described in Cemetery L were found but few were of special importance. One possible example of the sacred bark occurred (fig. 13f). The "granary" mark, so common in Cemetery L and well known elsewhere, was also found.[37] It had a nested meander pattern superimposed on it.[38] This particular design occurred twice in Cemetery W. For a second meander, see fig. 26b, and for others, see figs. 26a and 31c (amphibian?).

PAINTING ON EGYPTIAN AND A-GROUP POTTERY

The ovoid Egyptian storage jar with three lug handles on the shoulder (W 6—5) was decorated with red, painted designs. This decoration consists of a crudely crosshatched band on the shoulder, a palm with a V-shaped crown of radiating lines, and a trunk made of a single vertical line. Two wavy lines curve back and forth across the trunk. These lines probably show a simplified form of the intertwined serpents that appear on a number of objects from the Naqada period in Egypt. Both the application of Naqada II/Gerzean vertical lugs to this jar[39] and the palm and serpent decoration are important for our understanding of decorated pottery in Nubia and Egypt.[40]

A second vessel, a bowl from W 11 (8), which is a large and relatively rich tomb, is painted with four shapes which appear to be palms with V-shaped fronds and abbreviated trunks. Inside, lines spiral from the center to the rim. In shape, this bowl is an A-Group imitation of an Egyptian hard pink vessel. A similar imitation from L 17 was decorated with four solid palm-shapes outside and zigzag lines inside. The composition is probably a simplified version of the series of palm or tree-centered compositions painted on the great bowl from L 19. The comparison can also be extended to the single palm on the L 23 bowl and the standard on the L 6 jar. Like the seals discussed above, the painted bowls and jars from Qustul, with their variations of the palm motif, have numerous counterparts in the art of Nubia and Egypt during this period. These vessels form a stylistic and chronological cluster which allows a stage in the development of pharaonic art and symbolism to be identified and interpreted.[41]

F. THE A-GROUP AT QUSTUL

The A-Group remains discovered in Cemeteries W, V, S, and T are richer than those found in most A-Group sites. For example, more A-Group painted vessels were found in these burials than occur in much larger groups of cemeteries. However, the materials discussed in this volume do not differ as much from the average as those found in Cemetery L. Moreover, the cemeteries, though hardly crowding the desert edge, appear to have been

Figure 13. Potmarks: (a) W 10—17; (b) W 6—7; (c) W 19—2; (d) W 10—6; (e) W 10—9; (f) W 6—4; (g) W 11—2. Scale 2:5.

arranged hierarchically in relation to Cemetery L. To the north, Cemetery Q contained only cache pits. Cemetery W, just to the south of Q, contained a number of large, patrician type tombs with a still larger number of ordinary and even poor burials. Cemetery V, located even closer to Cemetery L, contained four very large tombs, which all may have had side chambers. There were also three circular pits which may have been made as cache pits. Two were reused for burials.

The A-Group loci found closest to Cemetery L were found in Cemetery S, just to the north and west. S 1-S 4 were not burials but a group of shafts located toward the south end of Cemetery S. One was reused for a later coffin burial, but no evidence of burials occurred otherwise. The essentially rectangular shapes of S 2-4 were quite unusual for storage pits, but the depression in the bottom of S 3 connects it with similar features found in round deposit pits. The orientations of the shafts are the same as the tombs in Cemetery L, and it is quite probable that these very large deposit holes were constructed as part of the nearby Cemetery L complex. A stone slab found in the fill of S 3, described in the records as roughly hewn, could very well have been part of a stela thrown into the shaft when it was reused as a burial. In the sketch of S 3 on the record sheet, it appears to have had parallel sides and a round top, a shape typical of stelae in Nubia and Egypt.

The late A-Group burials and deposits of Cemeteries W, V, S, and L are arranged hierarchically, an arrangement that has numerous, approximate parallels in the royal cemetery areas of Egypt. For the specific relationship between the deposits in Cemetery S and Cemetery L, see chapter 4 below.

G. REGISTER OF FINDS

The register is an extension of the recording on the Oriental Institute Nubian Expedition burial sheets. Apart from essential facts of burial and the shape of the tomb (with a simple sketch), the sheet lists objects found in the tomb, generally in order of their appearance. Sheets from tombs in Cemetery W, which were often intact, almost always list complete objects, but others often refer to items such as sherds which do not form complete objects but which could be individually identified. A small label identified each object with a number (for example, W 2—1) and information on the findspot within the tomb; these remarks were later used as the basis for describing the provenience in the field register. Proveniences given to individual objects identify the tomb of origin quite clearly, but the original location of scattered fragments within the tomb was often not indicated precisely. The register in 1962-63 identified individual objects and samples; sherds were identified only by tomb number and not registered separately; some complete vessels were not registered. In 1963-64, only objects were registered; material samples and sherds were identified only as coming from a certain locus. In some cases, relatively undistinguished small objects were considered samples. Both types of recording were encountered. Although the individual objects, sherds, and samples were clearly noted by location, entries on some burial sheets, such as "sherd sample taken," indicate that the recovery of sherds was not complete and was probably haphazard. A number of items were discarded at the end of the season or were left in the tombs. A vehicle accident that mixed up some of the sherds from Cemetery L did not affect materials presented in this volume although a few objects have not always been assigned to the proper tomb (see W 6-8 and W 11-8).

Tomb description: The entry gives the type of deposit, simplified description, and dimensions as recorded. Illustrations are cited at the right margin.

Burial: The position of the body is given according to a code indicated in table 17 below. Any minor modifications of the positions described by these codes and all occurrences of unusual positions will be explained in this entry. Most truly unusual positions were probably caused by disturbances such as tomb plundering.

Body: The age and sex of the body are given as they were recorded by members of the expedition. In 1963-64, the anthropologist was Duane Burnor. The categories used were infant I and II, juvenile, adult, mature, and senile. In doubtful cases, the categories are hyphenated. Sometimes, an estimate in years or months was indicated.

Objects: Apart from the burial and sherds, the contents of the tomb are listed under the heading "Objects." In cases where the the structure of the tomb was complex or the objects were arranged in some special way, there is a subheading that indicates the location of various objects within the tomb. Important individual objects are listed, generally in the numerical order established in the field. A few objects were added to this list in Chicago, and the numbers were sometimes changed for publication (the key number for any object is the OIM number [Oriental Institute Museum, Chicago]). Each object has a brief verbal descriptive designation, followed by the descriptive codes which are necessary to locate it in the appropriate discussion or table in the text of chapter 2; where the table is brief, codes are not indicated in the tomb register. Pottery is also indexed by an upper case roman letter which indicates its place in the series of vessels of its Form Group within the tomb. Where much of the pottery was in sherds, the Form Group series are listed at the end of the tomb entry. Each object has an OIM number, Cairo Museum number (*Journal d'entrée*), or it is designated as "sample," "sherds," or "discarded."

Pottery: Where separate lists of sherds are appended to the tomb entry, individual vessels are indicated by a roman letter, followed by the code that refers to the table in the text. In some Form Groups, the number of sherds or approximate proportion of the vessel is given, followed by other descriptive information: number within the tomb (where applicable), OIM number (where applicable), and illustration. On the line immediately below the entries of certain vessels are special remarks on decoration, potmarks, and Munsell color readings.

Table 17—Burial Codes

Orientation: this is given by the compass direction of the head:
    N, S, E, SE, etc.

Position: this is a series of codes beginning with a single letter indicating whether the body lay on its right (R) or left (L) side.

Legs:
    (1. legs straight)
    (2. legs slightly contracted, angle of thigh to back less than 20 deg.)
    Codes 1 and 2 were not used in the present work.
    3. legs partly contracted, thighs 20-45 deg.
    4. legs partly contracted, thighs 45-75 deg.
    5. legs semicontracted, thighs 75-90 deg.
    6. legs contracted, thighs 90-135 deg.
    7. legs tightly contracted, thighs over 135 deg.
    8. other

Arms and hands, codes only for burial on sides:
    a. arms extended straight before side
    b. arms bent, hands before base of pelvis
    c. arms bent, hands before upper pelvis or chest
    d. arms bent, hands before face
    e. arms bent, hands on face
    f. other

CEMETERY W

Cemeteries W 1 and W 2 consisted of clusters of tombs and cache pits found on the terrace ca. 1 km south of the great Qustul (Q) cemetery, just north of the village of Qustul (table 18). W1 began in Middle A-Group as a plot of burials with some round deposit holes just to the west. Ultimately, most of the forty-two numbered tombs in the main area were made during the A-Group period, and a few were made much later. There were about twenty-four unnumbered circular pits. These were probably originally cache pits, but a few were reused for burials.

Cemetery W 2 was actually three clusters of burials. That to the south contained about ten later graves with six round deposit holes probably of A-Group origin and two early burials of uncertain date. Both cemeteries were excavated between 25 February and 4 March 1964.

Table 18—Register of A-Group Graves in Cemetery W (pls. 2, 3a)

				FIGURE	PLATE
W 1	Dyn. XXV-Napatan				
W 2	Middle A-Group—Late A-Group transition			14	
	Shaft: rect. with rounded corners, 1.65 × .70 × .22 m N-S			14a	
	Burial: N/L/6/d				
	Body: —				
	Objects in shaft:				
	1. A-Group Exterior Painted bowl	I-A/38-39	A 24185	14f	16b
	2. A-Group fine bowl	VI *alpha*-E3a	A 24187	14g	21e
	3. Eight polished pebbles inside 2		24188		
	4. Palette form B and black grinding pebble		23847	14d	38e
	5. A-Group fine oval bowl (boat) (red burnish)	VI *alpha*-F	B 24094	14h	21a
	6. Ivory cylinder seal		23848	14b	13b
	7. Palette form B		23849	14c	38d
	8. Palette form A (triangular)		23850	14e	38f
	9. Black pebble inside 1		24186		
W 3	Late (?)				
W 4	No record (probably A-Group)				
W 5	A-Group			15	
	Shaft: rect. with rounded ends, 1.75 × .88 × .86 m			15a	
	Burial: S/L/5/d				
	Body: adult, probably female				

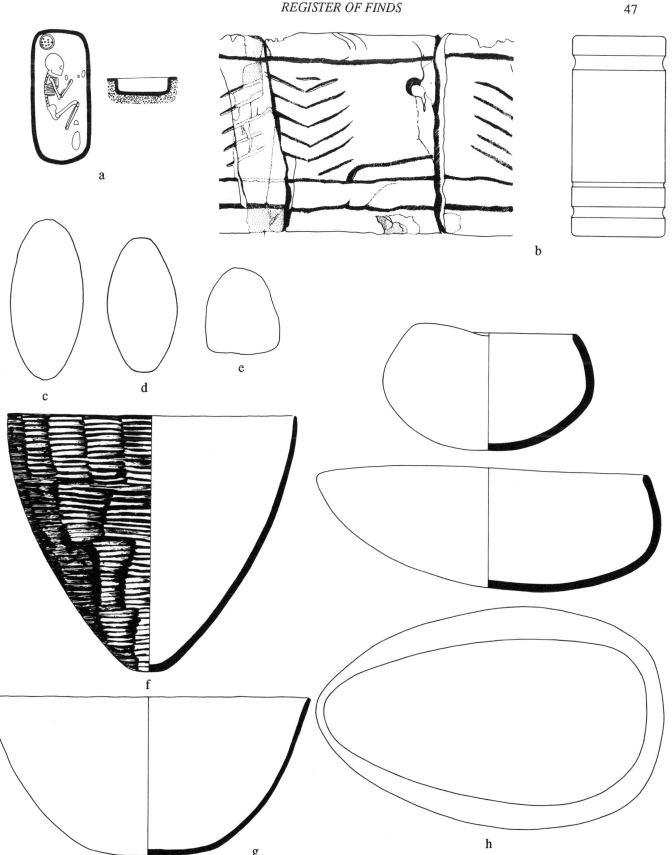

Figure 14. W 2: (a) Plan and section; (b) Cylinder Seal, no. 6; Palettes— (c) No. 7; (d) No. 4; (e) No. 8; Pottery— (f) No. 1; (g) No. 2; (h) No. 5. Scale 2:5 except (a) 1:50, (b) ca. 27:16.

Table 18—Register of A-Group Graves in Cemetery W — Cont.

				FIGURE	PLATE
W 5 — Cont.					
Objects in shaft:					
1. Egyptian jar	X-W	A 23965		15e	29c
2. A-Group coarse jar, five holes for mending	VI *gamma*-G	A 24258		15d	25b
3. A-Group coarse jar	VI *gamma*-K	B 23784		15c	
4. Palette form C, traces of malachite		23857		15b	38h
W 6 Middle A-Group				16-18	46a
Shaft: rect. with rounded ends, 1.86 × .80 × 1.05 m				16a	
Burials: A. disturbed					
B. S/R/7/d					
Bodies: A. —					
B. Adult female					
Objects in shaft:					
1. Bowl inverted over 2		disc.			
2. Egyptian jar	X-W	A 23770			
3. Egyptian coarse jar	XI-A	A 23779		17b	
4. Egyptian storage jar (marks, fig. 13f, 5YR 6/4, 2.5YR 6/4)	X-XIa	B 23768		18b	
5. Egyptian storage jar (painted decoration 2.5YR 5/4-6/4; surface 7.5YR7/4)	X-XIb	C 23766		18a	32a
6. A-Group coarse jar	VI *gamma*-K	A 23780		17c	
7. Egyptian bowl unburnished with potmark (mark fig. 13b)	X-Ml	D 23829		17a	28d
8. Egyptian bowl unburnished	X-F	E 24101		16i	26a
(For the painted bowl once assigned this provenience, see W 11-8)					
9. Palette form D and 3 grinding pebbles		23858		16b	38g
10. Clay incense model		24854			43d
11. Palette form C		23854		16c	38c
12. A-Group fine bowl (2.5YR 5/8 to grey, interior black)	VI *alpha* E1a	A 24162		16f	
13. A-Group fine bowl	VI *alpha*-Ela	B 23790		16e	21f
14. A-Group coarse bowl with red interior rim band	VI *gamma*-Al	B 24163		16h	23f
15. A-Group coarse bowl	VI *gamma*-E	B 23791		16g	23e
16. A-Group coarse cup	VI *gamma*-A2	C 23842		16d	22g
17. Five polished pebbles under skull A (?)		24856			44b

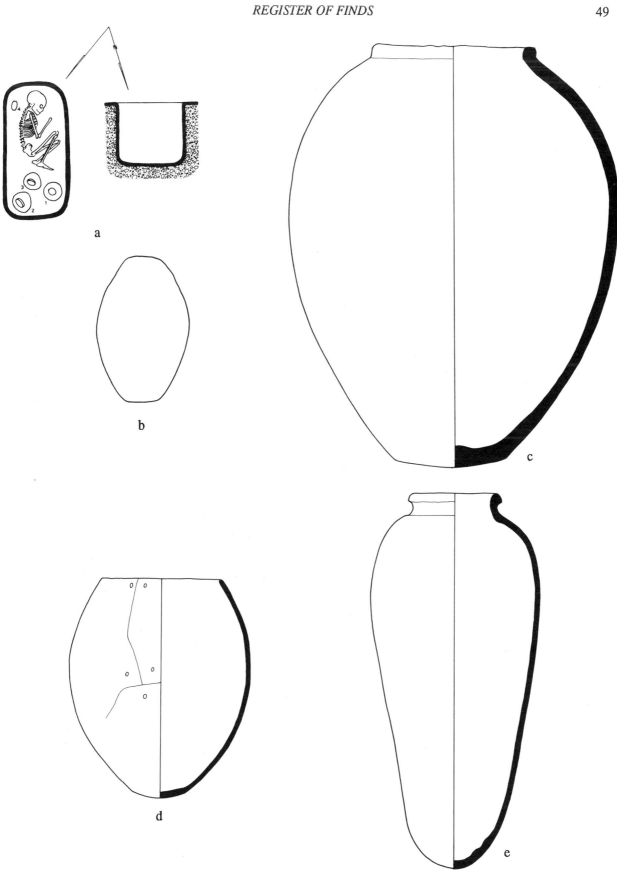

Figure 15. W 5: (a) Plan and section; (b) Palette, no. 4; Pottery— (c) No. 3; (d) No. 2; (e) No. 1. Scale 2:5 except (a) 1:50, (e) 1:5.

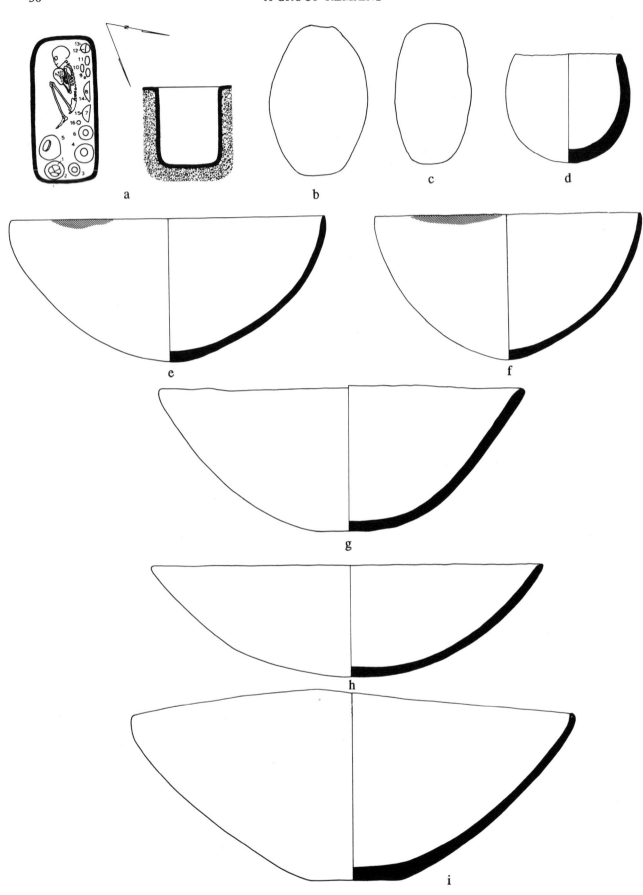

Figure 16. W 6: (a) Plan and section; Palettes— (b) No. 9; (c) No. 11; Pottery— (d) No. 16; (e) No. 13; (f) No. 12; (g) No. 15; (h) No. 14; (i) No. 8. Scale 2:5 except (a) 1:50.

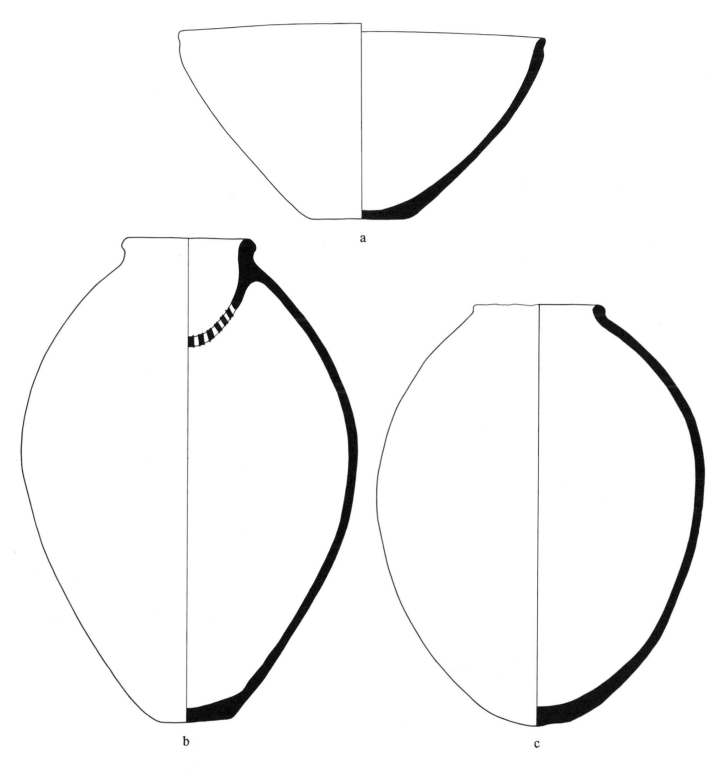

Figure 17. W 6: Pottery— (a) No. 7; (b) No. 3; (c) No. 6. Scale 2:5.

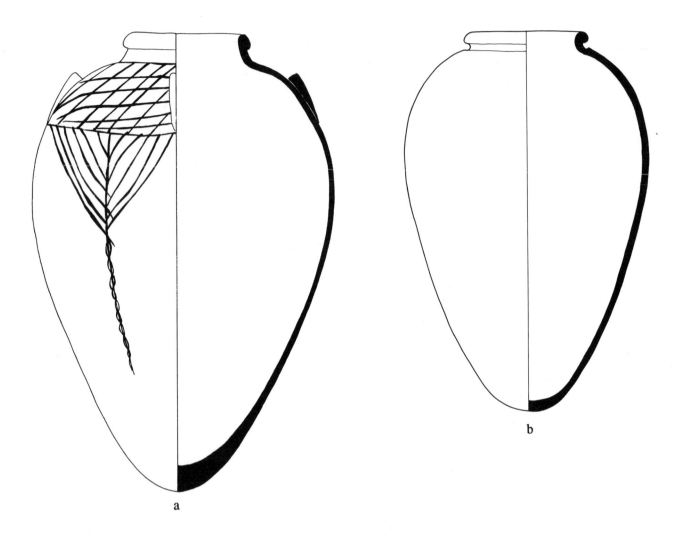

Figure 18. W 6: Pottery— (a) No. 5; (b) No. 4. Scale 1:5.

Table 18—Register of A-Group Graves in Cemetery W — Cont.

	FIGURE	PLATE
Southwest of W 6		
Sherds:		
1. Egyptian coarse stand or box XI C (rect.)	19	
W 7 A-Group	20	
Shaft: rect. with rounded ends, 2.00 × .80 × .65 m	20a	
Burials: A. S/R/7/d		
B. N/L/7/d		
Bodies: A. Adult female		
B. Adult male (?)		

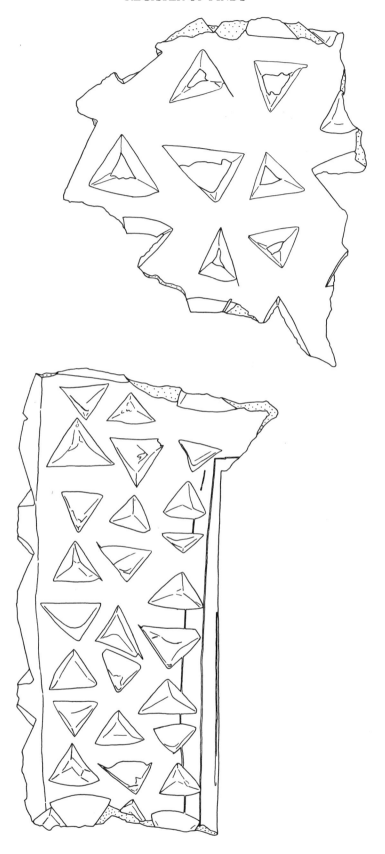

Figure 19. Two sherds of rectangular stands or boxes from SW of W 6. Scale 2:5.

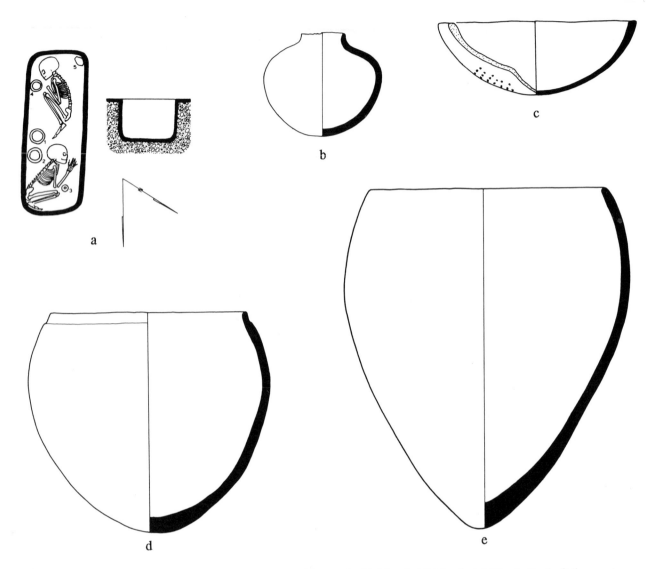

Figure 20. W 7: (a) Plan and section; Pottery— (b) No. 3; (c) No. 6; (d) No. 2; (e) No. 1. Scale 2:5 except (a) 1:50.

Table 18—Register of A-Group Graves in Cemetery W — Cont.

				FIGURE	PLATE
W 7 — Cont.					
Objects in shaft:					
1. A-Group coarse vessel	VI *gamma*-D	A 23789		20e	24a
2. A-Group coarse jar	VI *gamma*-C	B 24189		20d	
3. A-Group miniature (7.5YR 6/4)	VI *beta*-C	A 24080		20b	22h
4. Sherds		n/a			
5. Palette form A		24241			38a
6. Strainer	VI *alpha*-G	C 24859		20c	

Table 18—Register of A-Group Graves in Cemetery W — Cont.

				FIGURE	PLATE
W 8 Transition to Late A-Group				21	
Shaft: rect. with rounded ends, 1.80 × .95 × .80 m				21a	
Burial: W (N ?)/1/6/d					
Body: adult female					
Objects in shaft:					
1. A-Group coarse jar	VI *gamma*-H	A 23785		21e	
2. A-Group rippled bowl	II C	A 24102		21d	19c
(2.5YR5/6, patches of grey, grey-black interior)					
3. A-Group miniature (5YR 6/4)	VI *beta*-B	A 23778		21c	22i
4. Palette form A		24242		21b	
5. Grinding pebble		samp.			
W 9 A-Group				22	
Pit and Chamber: pit dimensions n/a, chamber, 1.15 × 1.50 × .50 m					
Burials: —					
Bodies: A. Child, less than 13, possibly ca. 6 years					
B. Adult, probably female					
C. Adult, possibly female					
Objects from chamber:					
1. Palette and 3 grinding pebbles		23855			39d
(shape unclassified)					
2. A-Group fine cup VI *alpha*-E1b		A 23951			23b
3. A-Group bowl, red with black interior (rippled?)		disc.			
4. A-Group jar, probably coarse	VI *gamma* (?)	disc.			
W 10 Late A-Group				23-26	46b
Shaft: rect. with rounded corners, 2.63 × 1.20 × .95 m fig. 23a					
Burial: S/R/7/d					
Body: adult female					
Objects in shaft:					
1. A-Group Exterior Painted bowl	I-A/174	A 24194		23e	16c
(2.5YR 4/8-5YR 6/4)					
2. A-Group Exterior Painted bowl	I-A/7	B 24151		23g	14e
3. A-Group Exterior Painted bowl	I-A/4	C 24161		23f	15a
4. A-Group Exterior Painted bowl	I-B/32	D 23771			15d
5. Egyptian storage jar,	X-X1a	A 23763		26b	31a
painted, potmark					

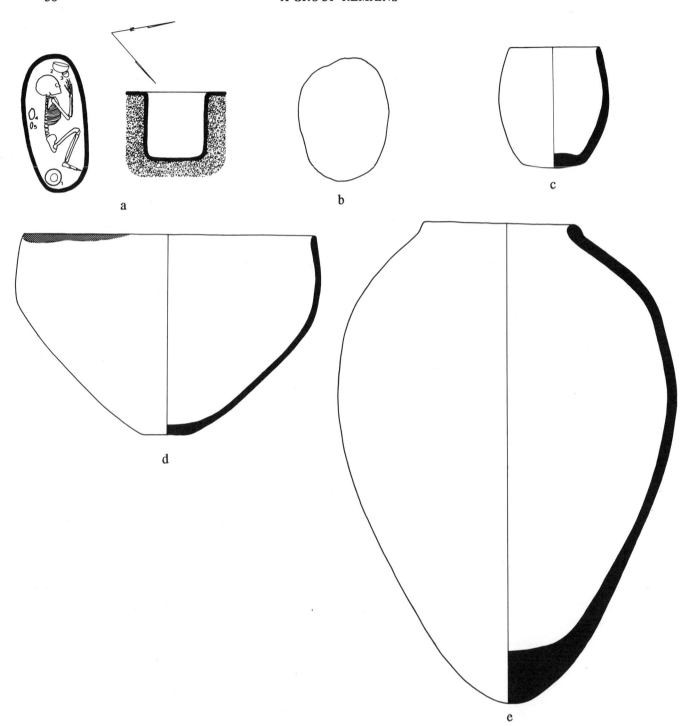

Figure 21. W 8: (a) Plan and section; (b) Palette, no. 4; Pottery— (c) No. 3; (d) No. 2; (e) No. 1. Scale 2:5 except (a) 1:50.

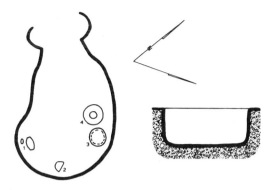

Figure 22. W 9, plan. Scale 1:50.

Table 18—Register of A-Group Graves in Cemetery W — Cont.

					FIGURE	PLATE
W 10 — Cont.						
6.	Egyptian bowl	X-C	B	24071	24f	28a
	(mark fig. 13d, 5YR 6/4 burnish strokes 2.5YR 6/8)					
7.	Egyptian storage jar (5YR 6/4)	X-X1a potmarks	C	23767	26a	30b
8.	Egyptian narrow jar	X-W	D	23769	26c	
9.	Egyptian bowl (marks, fig. 13e)	X-C deformed	E	23781	24e	
10.	Egyptian bowl containing 22	X-E	F	24049	25a	26e
11.	A-Group fine bowl	VI *alpha*-C1	A	24184	24d	
	(7.5YR 6/4 patches grey to black)					
12.	A-Group Exterior Painted bowl	I-B/4	E	24070	23c	14a
13.	A-Group Exterior Painted bowl	I-A/173	F	24120	23d	16d
14.	A-Group fine jar	VI *alpha*-A	B	23777	24a	22a
15.	A-Group Exterior Painted bowl	I-A/G field no.	B	1426		
		Cairo		89985		
16.	Palette form D, malachite			23856	23b	39c
17.	Egyptian bowl (mark, fig. 13a)	X-E	G	24050	25b	26c
18.	Grinding pebble (?)			n/a		
19.	Egyptian bowl	X-M2	H	24100	25d	27
	(2.5YR 6/6-2.5YR 5/8)					
20.	Egyptian bowl	X-E	I	24133	25c	26d
21.	A-Group miniature	VI *beta*-A	A	24081	24b	22e
	(red coat and burnish)					
22.	Red ochre from 10 above			24246		
23.	A-Group miniature	VI *beta*-A	B	24195	24c	22f
	(red coat and burnish)					

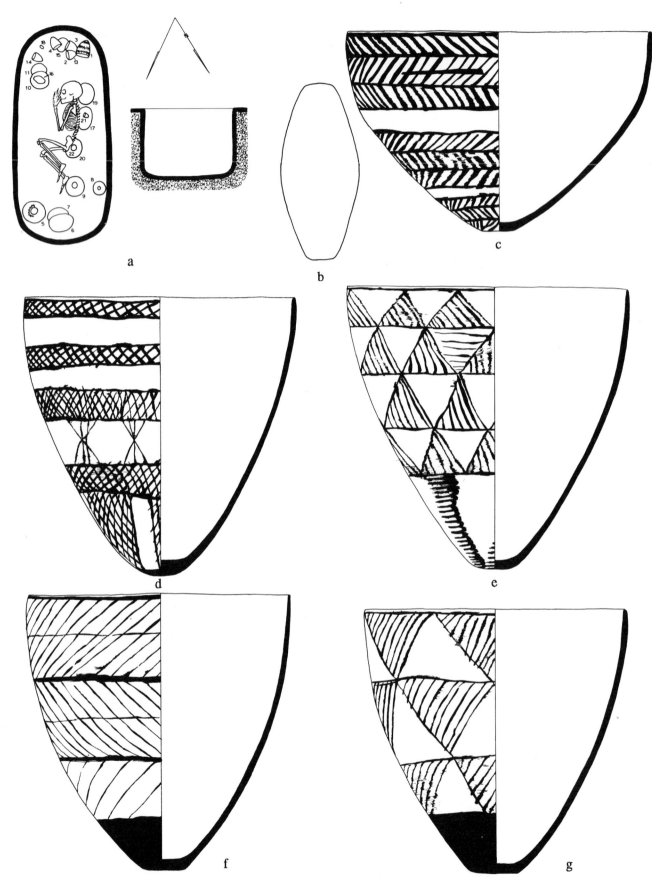

Figure 23. W 10: (a) Plan and section; (b) Palette, no. 16; Pottery— (c) No. 12; (d) No. 13; (e) No. 1; (f) No. 3; (g) No. 2. Scale 2:5 except (a) 1:50.

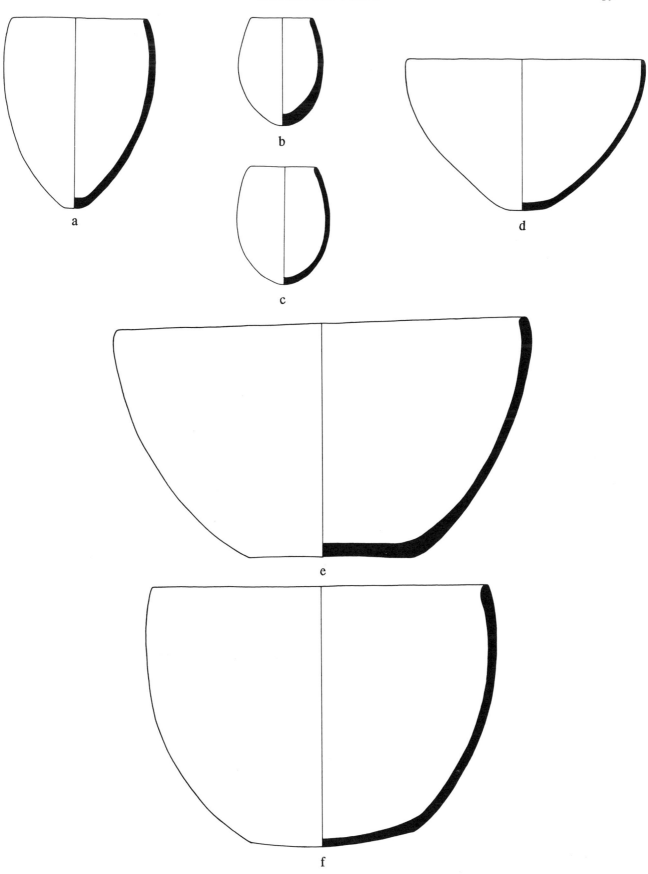

Figure 24. W 10: Pottery— (a) No. 14; (b) No. 21; (c) No. 23; (d) No. 11; (e) No. 9; (f) No. 6. Scale 2:5.

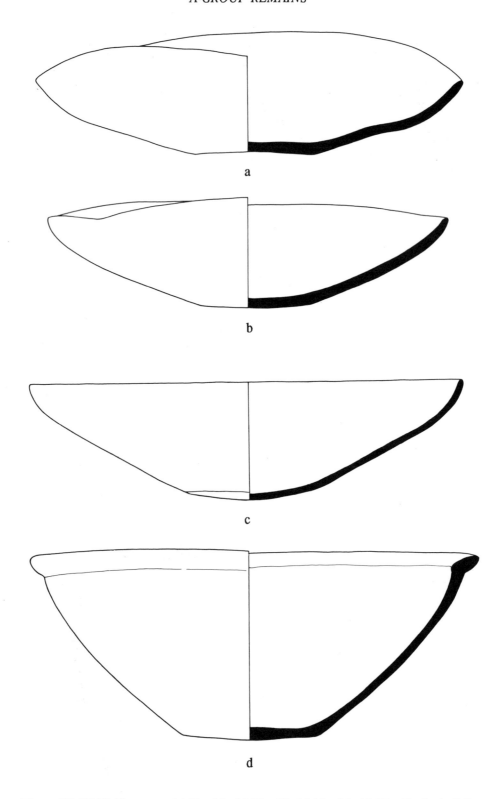

Figure 25. W 10: Pottery— (a) No. 10; (b) No. 17; (c) No. 20; (d) No. 19. Scale 2:5.

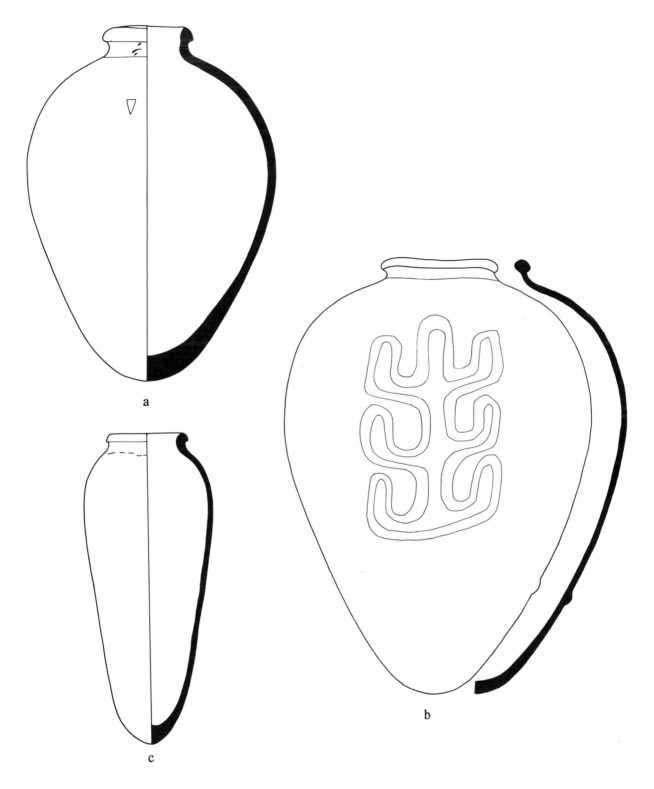

Figure 26. W 10: Pottery— (a) No. 7; (b) No. 5; (c) No. 8. Scale 1:5.

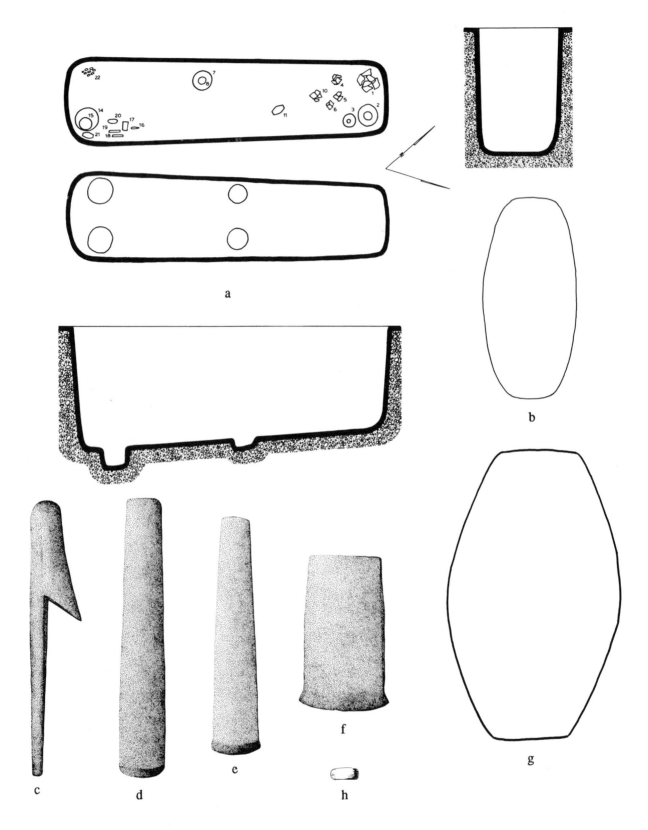

Figure 27. W 11: (a) Plan and sections; (b) Palette, no. 11; Copper implements— (c) No. 16; (d) No. 18; (e) No. 19; (f) No. 17; (g) Palette, no. 20; (h) Bead, no. 23. Scale 2:5 except (a) 1:50, (h) 4:5.

Table 18—Register of A-Group Graves in Cemetery W — Cont.

				FIGURE	PLATE
W 11 Transition to Late A-Group				27-31	

Shaft: rect. 4.30 × 1.10 × 1.35-1.64 m; 4 holes, two at center, two at S corners, for the bed burial.
Distance separating holes to N, 1.25 m, to S, 1.05 m. Holes, 15-25 cm deep. Above, to NE is a groove,
30 cm wide, 15 cm deep.   27a

Burial: bed

Body: —

Objects in shaft:

				FIGURE	PLATE
1. Egyptian storage jar	X-Xla	A	23765	31c	30c
2. Egyptian storage jar (marks fig. 13g)	X-Xla potmarks	B	23764	31b	31b
3. A-Group coarse jar	VI *gamma*-K	A	23783	30a	25a
4. A-Group Exterior Painted bowl	I-A/32	A	24148	28a	15e
5. A-Group Exterior Painted bowl	I-A/82	B	24121	28d	17b
6. A-Group Exterior Painted bowl	I-A/6	C	24170	28c	14d
7. Large undecorated pot			disc.		
8. A-Group Interior Painted bowl (The bowl is not classified; 5YR 6/6-2.5YR 4/6; for the attribution of this bowl to W 6 see note 14.)	V-	A	23772	29d	33
9. A-Group rippled cup (5 YR 6/6-2.5YR 5/6)	II-D	A	24150	28e	19a
10. A-Group Exterior Painted bowl	I-A/46	D	24169	28b	15b
11. Palette form C			23866	27b	38i
12. A-Group fine bowl	VI *alpha*-E3a	A	23773	29c	21b
13. Egyptian bowl (7.5YR 6/4)	X-G	C	24097	30b	
14. A-Group rippled bowl	II-B	C	24056	29a	
15. A-Group rippled bowl (2/5YR 4/6)	II-F	B	24149	28f	19e
16. Copper harpoon head			23870	27c	37a
17. Copper ax			23871	27f	37d
18. Copper adze			23872	27d	37c
19. Copper adze			23873	27e	37b
20. Palette form D, malachite			23869	27g	39f
21. A-group coarse jar (in SE hole)	VI *gamma*-L	B	23787	31a	
22. Pebbles from SW corner			samp.		
23. Discoid beads, tooth, size 2, 59			23867	27h	37m
24. A-Group miniature	VI *beta*-A	A	24257	29b	

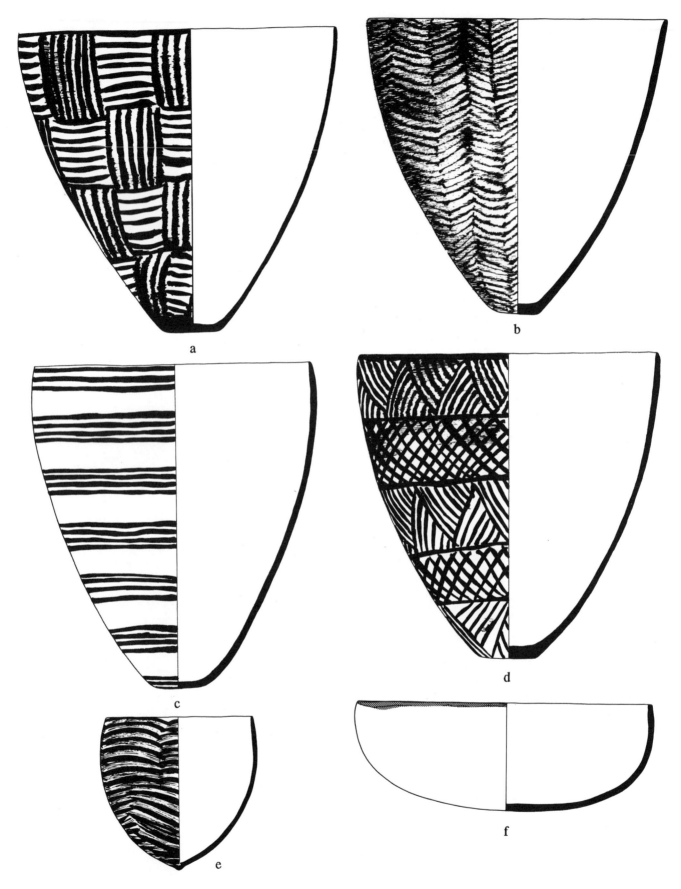

Figure 28. W 11: Pottery— (a) No. 4; (b) No. 10; (c) No. 6; (d) No. 5; (e) No. 9; (f) No. 15. Scale 2:5.

Figure 29. W 11: Pottery— (a) No. 14; (b) No. 24; (c) No. 12; (d) No. 8. Scale 2:5.

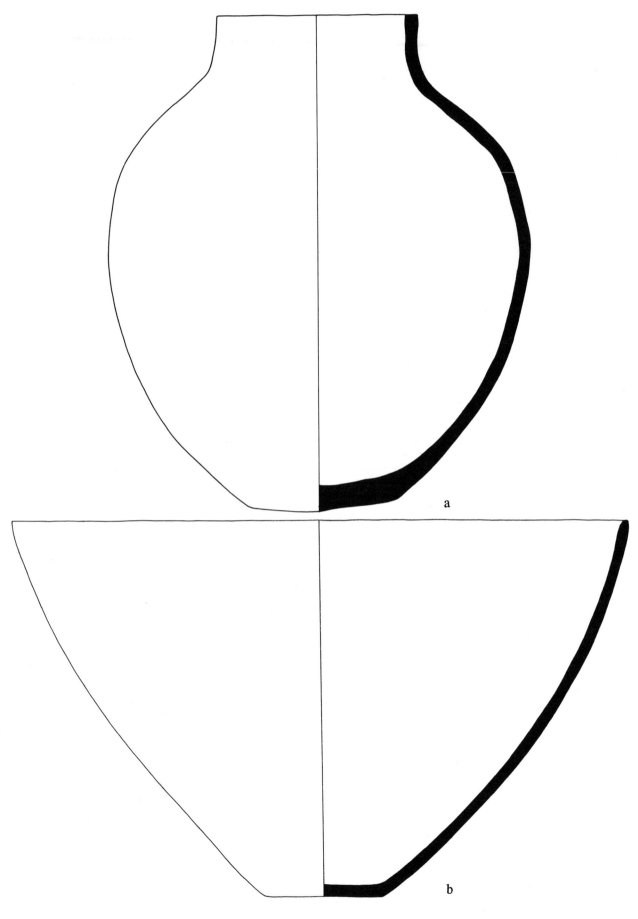

Figure 30. W 11: Pottery— (a) No. 3; (b) No. 13. Scale 2:5.

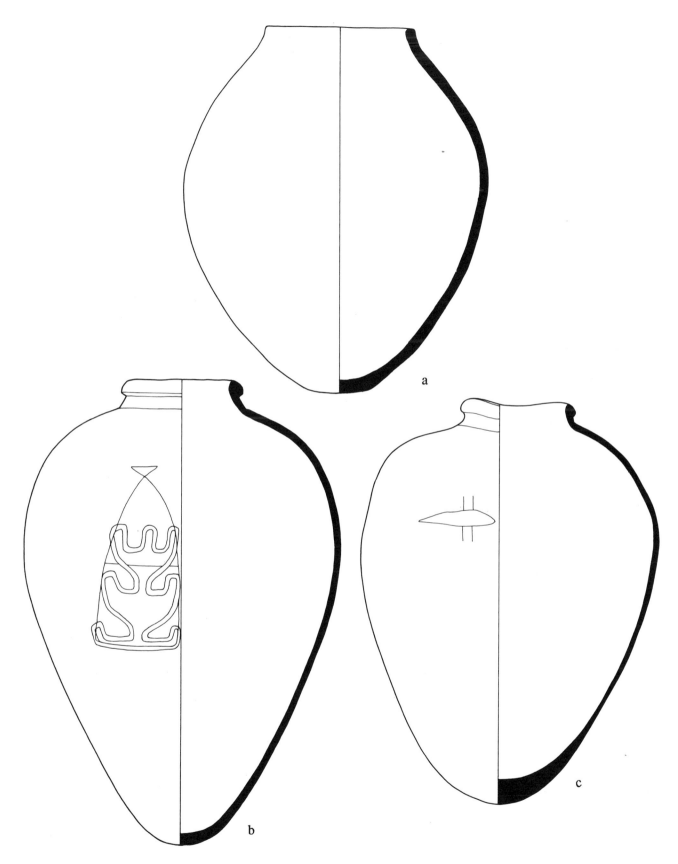

Figure 31. W 11: Pottery— (a) No. 21; (b) No. 2; (c) No. 1. Scale 1:5 except (a) 2:5.

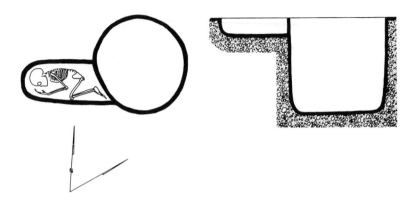

Figure 32. W 12: Plan and section. Scale 1:50.

Table 18—Register of A-Group Graves in Cemetery W — Cont.

				FIGURE	PLATE
W 12	A-Group			32	
	Shaft cut deposit pit: pit: 1.30 × 1.30 m; shaft: 1.20 × .60 × .35 m				
	Burial: W/R/6/d-e				
	Body: adult female				
	Objects: —				
W 13	Late (?)				
W 14	A-Group				
	Shaft and chamber: shaft: 1.65 × .80 × .50 m; chamber: 1.00 × 1.00 m				
	Burial: —				
	Objects: —				
W 15	Middle A-Group			33	
	Shaft: rect. with rounded corners, 1.70 × .70 × .65 m			33a	
	Burial: W (S?)/L/4/e, possibly disturbed				
	Body: adult female				
	Objects from shaft:				
	1. A-Group coarse jar	VI *gamma*-I	A 23782	33c	
	(2.5YR 5/8- 7.5 YR 7/4, rim and interior grey to black)				
	2. A-Group fine cup	VI *alpha*-E2	A 23832	33b	23a
	3. Palette form A (?) natural stone		24857		
	4. A-Group rippled bowl	II-E	A 24164	33e	19b
	5. A-Group rippled bowl	II-A	B 24134	33d	19f
	6. Two fragments of malachite under jaw		24858		

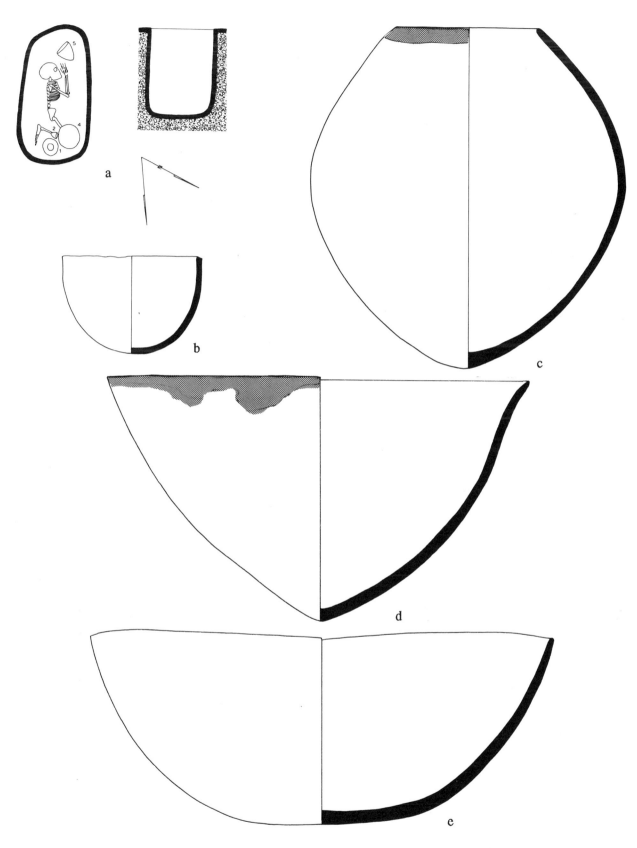

Figure 33. W 15: (a) Plan and section; Pottery— (b) No. 2; (c) No. 1; (d) No. 5; (e) No. 4. Scale 2:5 except (a) 1:50.

Table 18—Register of A-Group Graves in Cemetery W (pls. 2, 3a) — Cont.

			FIGURE	PLATE
W 16 A-Group				
Shaft: oval, 1.70 × .90 × .40 m				
Burial: —				
Body: —				
Objects from shaft:				
1. A-Group coarse jar	VI *gamma*-F	A 23831	37a	24c
W 17 A-Group				
Shaft: rect. 1.40 × .80 × .40 m				
Burial: —				
Body: adult, probably male				
Objects from shaft:				
1. Sherds		disc.		
W 18 No record, probably A-Group				
W 19 Late A-Group			34-36	
Shaft: rect. with rounded corners, 2.40 × 1.32 × .63 m;			47b	
two holes along center axis of bottom:				
A. .39 × .14 m; B. .29 × .17 m			34a	
Burial: SW (S)/R (?)/4(?)/— disturbed				
Body: adult female				
Objects in shaft:				
1. Egyptian coarse jar	XI-A	A 24044	36a	32b
2. Egyptian storage jar	X-X2	A 23825	36b	30a
(mark fig. 13c)				
3. A-Group miniature	VI *beta*-A	A 23837	35d	22d
4. A-Group Exterior Painted bowl	I-B/4	A 24048	35b	14b
(2.5YR 4/4, 2.5YR 5/6)				
5. A-Group fine bowl	VI *alpha*-E3b	A 24068	35f	21c
6. Incense Burner form A (sandstone)		23875	34e	
7. Quartzite mortar form C and quartz pestle		23874	34f	36e
8. Palette form D		23861	34b	39a
9. Discoid beads: size 1		23501	34d	41e
a. Car.	} 344			37o
b. Gar.				37o
c. Blue fai.	53			37k-1
10. A-Group fine bowl	VI *alpha*-E3c	B 24067	35g	21d

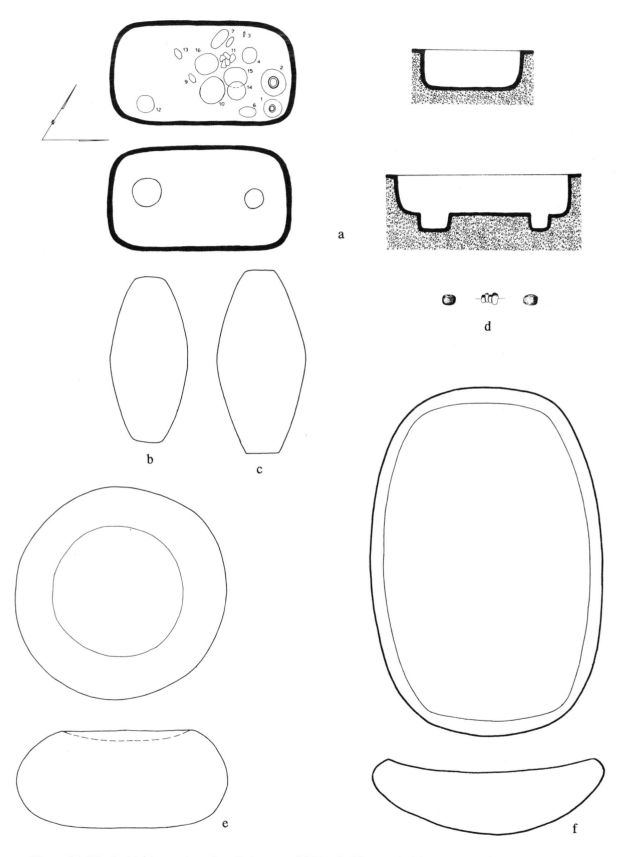

Figure 34. W 19: (a) Plan and section; Palettes— (b) No. 8; (c) No. 13; (d) Beads, no. 9; (e) Incense burner, no. 6; (f) Mortar, no. 7. Scale 2:5 except (a) 1:50 and (d) 4:5.

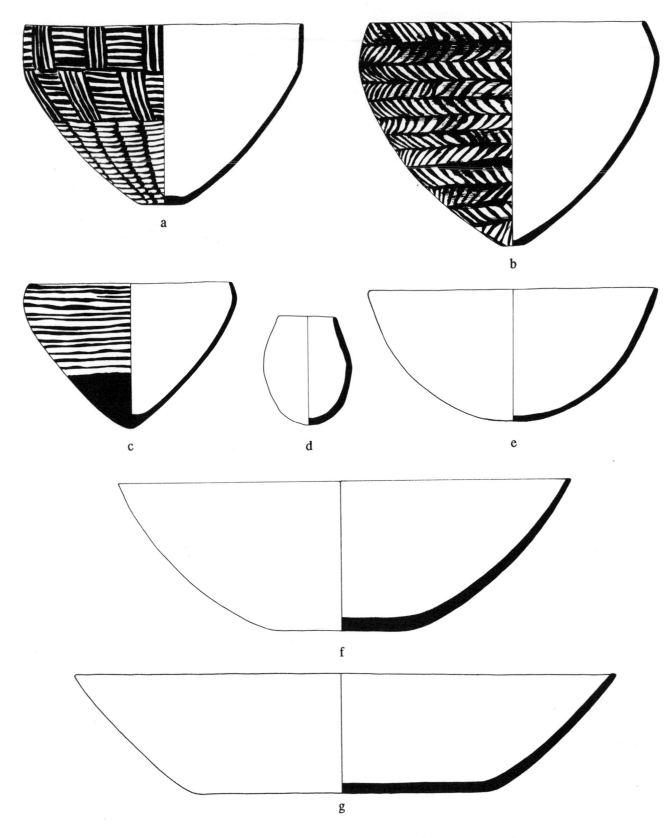

Figure 35. W 19: Pottery— (a) No. 15; (b) No. 4; (c) No. 12; (d) No. 3; (e) No. 14; (f) No. 5; (g) No. 10.
Scale 2:5.

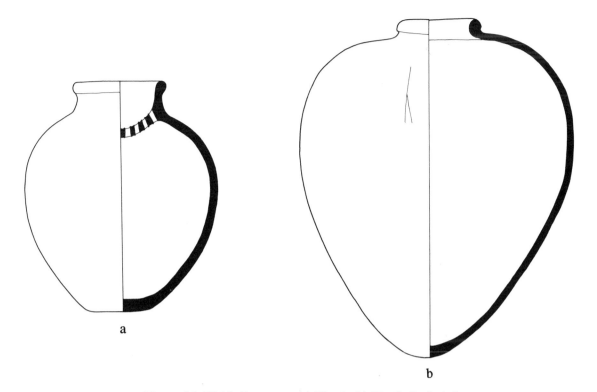

Figure 36. W 19: Pottery— (a) No. 1; (b) No. 2. Scale 1:5.

Table 18—Register of A-Group Graves in Cemetery W — Cont.

			FIGURE	PLATE
W 19 — Cont.				
Objects in shaft:				
11. A-Group Exterior Painted bowl 1-B/2	B 24871			
(2.5YR 4/6, 2.5YR 6/6, areas near rim and interior grey to black)				
12. A-Group Exterior Painted bowl I-B/6 (pierced point)				
(2.5YR3/4-5YR 6/4, 5YR 2.5/1)	C 24045		35c	14c
13. Palette form D	23862		34c	39b
14. A-Group fine bowl VI *alpha*-E1a	C 24872		35e	
15. A-Group Exterior Painted bowl I-B/32	D 24051		35a	15c
16. Egyptian bowl X-L	24046			28c
W 20 Possibly A-Group				

Shafts: A. circular pit .71 × .88 × .43; cut by B. oval shaft: .66 × .35 × .10–.18 m
Burial: N/L/5/— disturbed in oval shaft
Body: infant, less than 1 year
Objects in shaft:

1. Discoid beads:	23860	41a
a. ost. or other egg. small size 1 (3 mm) 111		
b. blue fai. size 1 4		
c. gn. fai. size 1 1		

Note that the eggshell beads are thinner than normal ostrich egg., ca. 1 mm.

Table 18—Register of A-Group Graves in Cemetery W — Cont.

				FIGURE	PLATE
W 21 Middle A-Group					47a
Shaft: rect. with rounded ends, $1.05 \times .75 \times .48$ m					
Burial: NW (N)/1/—/c disturbed					
Body: ca. 10 years, female?					
Objects in shaft:					
1. A-Group rippled bowl	II-C		24191	37b	19d
W 22 Middle A-Group					
Shaft: rect. with rounded ends, $.85 \times .56 \times .25$ m					
Burial: dist.					
Body: probably child					
Objects in shaft:					
1. Egyptian wavy-handled jar (5YR 7/6)	X-P	A	23774	37c	28b
Painted marks (10R 4/6)					
2. Beads:			23863	37d	41b
a. car., ca. 1×4 mm	2				37n
b. tooth, ca. 9×7 mm	1				37j
c. agate (red bands), ca. 7×3 mm	38				37n
d. serpentine ca. 9×4 mm	6				
e. blue fai. balls, ca. 8×6	2				
f. blue-gn. fai. notched, ca. 10×4.5 mm	12				37 f, g
g. basalt?, ca. 7×3 mm	3				37n
h. crystal pendant, ca. $10 \times 8 \times 4$ mm	1				37h
i. steatite pendant, broken	1				
W 23 Middle A-Group				38	48b
Shaft: rect. with rounded ends $1.43 \times .55 \times .65$ m				38a-b	
Burials: A. S/R/5/d					
B. S/R/6/d					
Bodies: A. Adult female					
B. Mature female					
Objects in shaft:					
1. A-Group coarse jar	VI *gamma*-J	A	23826	38i	
2. A-Group fine bowl	VI *alpha*-D	A	24190	38e	23h
3. A-Group rippled bowl	II-E	A	24093	38f	
4. A-Group coarse jar (5YR 6/6)	VI *gamma*-K	B	23925	38h	
5. Badly broken, large jar				disc.	
6. Palette form D			23971	38d	
7. A-Group coarse jar	VI *gamma*-K	C	23786	38g	24d
8. Palette, unclassified form			23652	38c	

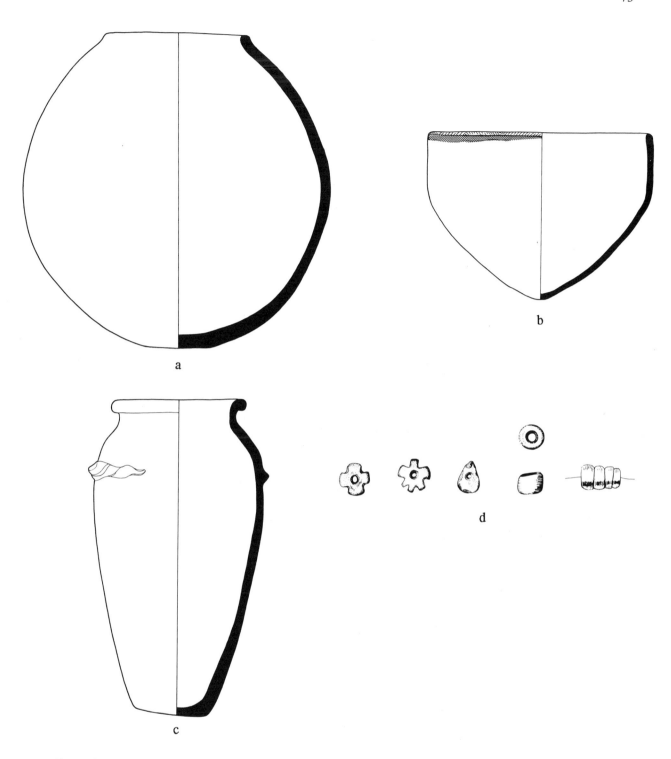

Figure 37. Pottery and beads from W 16, W 21, and W 22: Pottery— (a) W 16—1; (b) W 21—1; (c) W 22—1; (d) Beads, W 22—2. Scale 2:5 except (d) 4:5.

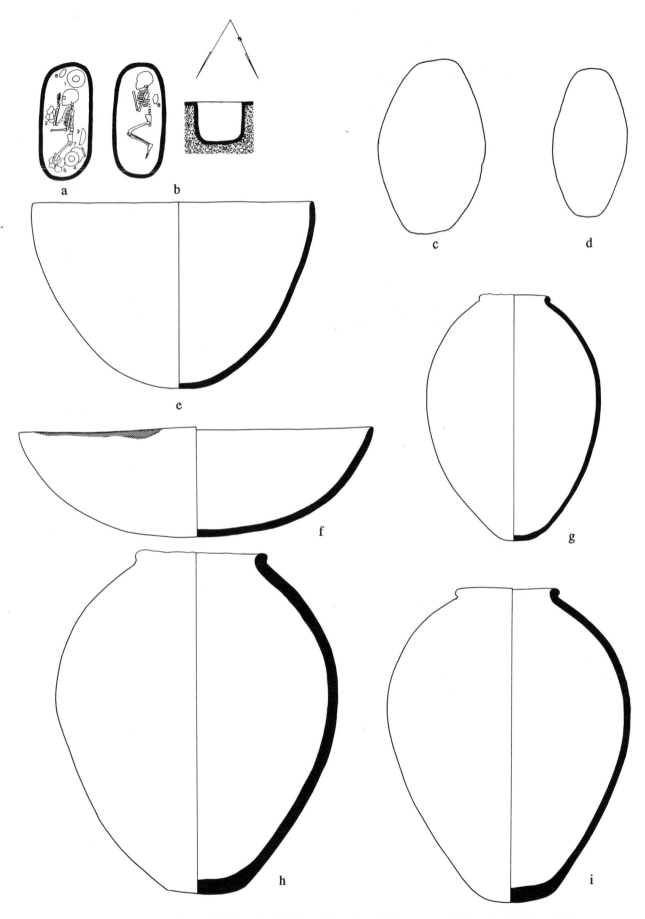

Figure 38. W 23: (a) Plan; (b) Plan, burial B, and section; Palettes— (c) No. 8; (d) No. 6; Pottery—
(e) No. 2; (f) No. 3; (g) No. 7; (h) No. 4; (i) No. 1. Scale 2:5 except (a), (b) 1:50, (g) 1:5.

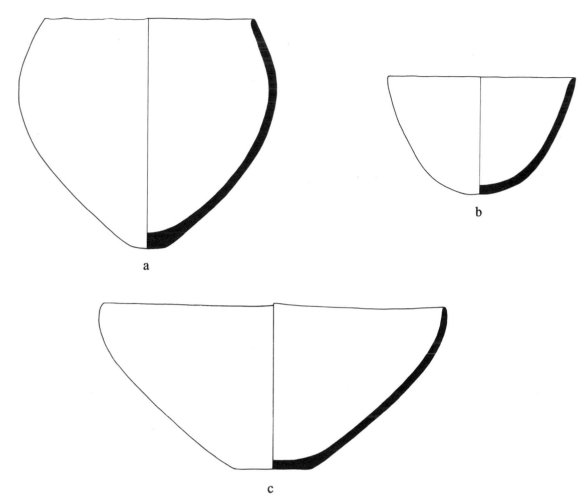

Figure 39. Pottery from W 25, W 27, and W 31: (a) W 25—1; (b) W 27—1; (c) W 31—1. Scale 2:5.

Table 18—Register of A-Group Graves in Cemetery W — Cont.

				FIGURE	PLATE
W 24 Dyn. XXV-Napatan					
W 25 A-Group					
Shaft: rect. with rounded ends, 1.02 × .45 × .55 m					
Burial: N/R/5/d					
Body: child, probably female					
Objects in shaft:					
1. A-Group fine bowl	VI *alpha*-C2	A 23788	39a		23g

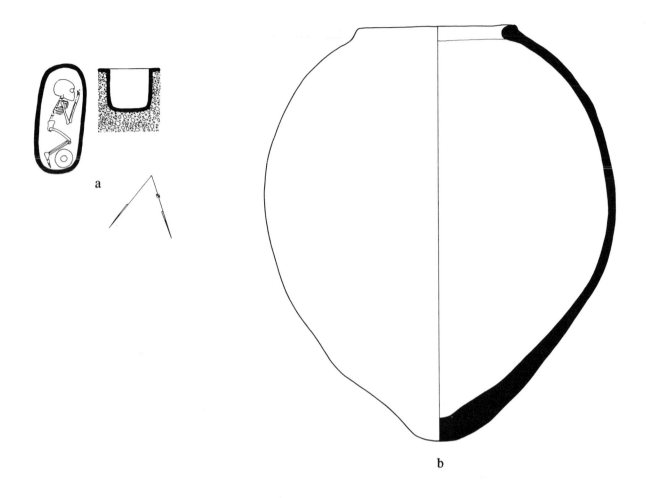

Figure 40. W 26: (a) Plan and section; (b) Jar, no. 1. Scale (a) 1:50, (b) 2:5.

Table 18—Register of A-Group Graves in Cemetery W — Cont.

				FIGURE	PLATE
W 26	A-Group				
	Shaft: rect. with rounded ends, $1.38 \times .72 \times .50$ m			40a	48a
	Burial: N/R/6/d				
	Body: 3-6 years				
	Objects in shaft:				
	1. A-Group coarse jar	VI *gamma*-H	A 23830	40b	24b

Table 18—Register of A-Group Graves in Cemetery W — Cont.

		FIGURE	PLATE

W 27 A-Group
 Shaft: oval, .70 × .55 × .23 m
 Burial: S/L/6/d(?) disturbed
 Body: ca. 6 1/2 years
 Objects in shaft:

1. A-Group fine bowl (5YR 6/3) VI *alpha*-D	A 24135	39b	23c

W 28 A-Group pit, late shaft
 Shafts: A. late oval infant burial
 B. circular pit cut by A, diam. ca. .60 m
 Objects: —

W 29 A-Group
 Shaft: oval, 1.20 × 1.70 × .43 m
 Burial: N/R/—/d(?) disturbed
 Body: 3-6 years
 Objects in shaft:

1. Beads (the colors vary and blend, total 514);	23859	41d

 all are discoid, sizes 1-2, roughly graduated
 a. blue fai.
 b. gn. fai.

W 30 A-Group
 Shaft: oval, 1.15 × .75 × .33 m
 Burial: S/L/6/d
 Body: adult male
 Objects: —

W 31 A-Group   49b
 Shaft: rect. with rounded corners, 1.88 × 1.00 × .65 m
 Burial: S/L/6/d
 Body: adult female
 Objects in shaft:

1. Egyptian bowl	X-F	A 23834	39c	26b
2. Seeds, possibly durra		samp.		

Table 18—Register of A-Group Graves in Cemetery W — Cont.

				FIGURE	PLATE
W 32 A-Group				41	49a
Shaft: rect. with rounded ends, $1.68 \times .73 \times .65$ m				41a	
Burials:	A.	W/L/6/d			
	B.	Scattered bones under A			
Bodies:	A.	Adult, possibly male			
	B.	Child, 2-3 years			
Objects in shaft:					
	1.	Egyptian jar (5YR 6/4)	X-W	A 23827	41e	29a
	2.	Egyptian jar	X-W	B 23828	41f	29b
	3.	A-Group fine bowl	VI *alpha*-B1	A 24099	41c	22b
	4.	A-Group fine bowl (5 YR 6/4)	VI *alpha*-A	B 23775	41d	22c
	5.	A-Group coarse cup	VI *gamma*-B	A 23776	41b	23d
	6.	Six polished pebbles		24861		44a
	7.	Sherds of red flat bowl		disc.		
W 33 A-Group					
Shaft: rect. with rounded ends, $1.20 \times .62 \times 1.00$ m					
Burial: S/L/6/d disturbed					
Body: adult female					
Objects in shaft:					
	1.	A-Group coarse jar	VI *gamma*-J	A 23924	42b	
	2.	Palette form C		23868	42a	38b
W 34 Late					
W 35 A-Group					
Shaft: rect. with rounded ends, $1.00 \times .75 \times .25$ m					
Burial: S/R/5/c					
Body: 12-13 years, probably female					
Objects in shaft: —					
W 36 Late					
W 37 Late					
W 38 A-Group					43	
Shaft: rect. with rounded ends, $1.20 \times .60 \times .45$ m					43a	
Burial: S/R/5/d					
Body: 8-9 years, possibly female					
Objects in shaft:					
	1.	Large jar		disc.		
	2.	Sudanese incised bowl	VII	A 24047	43c	
	3.	Palette form D and grinding pebble, malachite		23876	43b	39e
	4.	Copper awl in bone handle		24247		13c

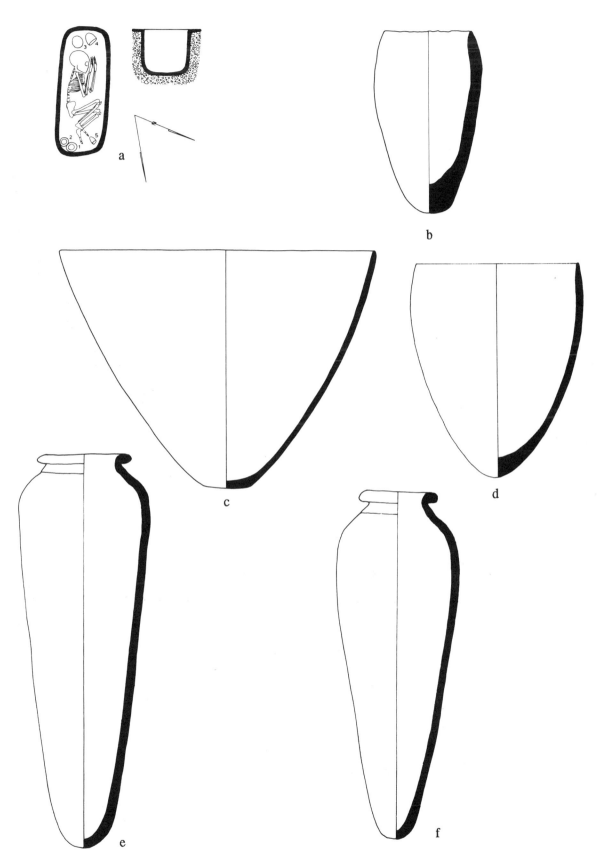

Figure 41. W 32: (a) Plan and section; Pottery— (b) No. 5; (c) No. 3; (d) No. 4; (e) No. 1; (f) No. 2. Scale 2:5 except (a) 1:50, (e), (f) 1:5.

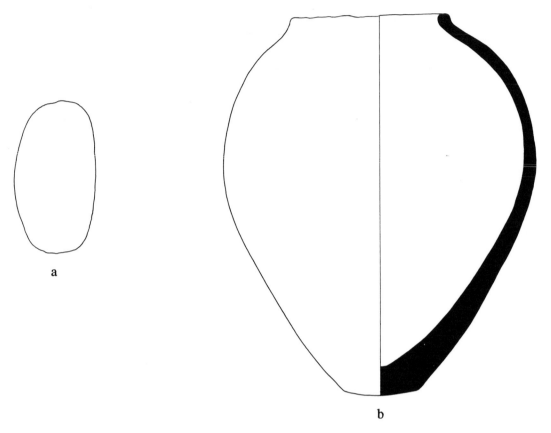

Figure 42. W 33: (a) Palette, no. 2; (b) Jar, no. 1. Scale 2:5.

Table 18—Register of A-Group Graves in Cemetery W — Cont.

	FIGURE	PLATE
W 39 A-Group shaft (?), late intrusive burial		
W 40-71 Dyn. XXV-Napatan and later		
W 72 A-Group (?)	44a	
Shaft: rect. with rounded ends, 2.12 × 1.25 × 1.30 m		
Burial: S/L/6/— disturbed; stones around and below body;		
3 holes for beams in each wall, 2 close to top,	44b, c	
1 near bottom of pit		
Body: adult male		
Objects: —		

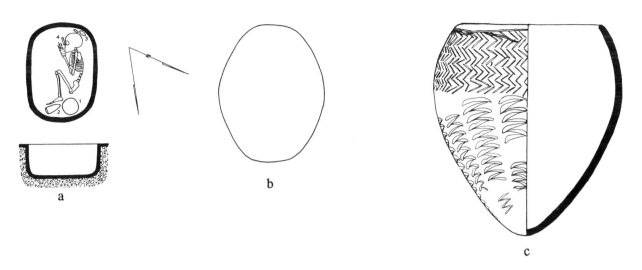

Figure 43. W 38: (a) Plan and section; (b) Palette, no. 3; (c) Bowl, no. 2. Scale 2:5 except (a) 1:50.

Table 18—Register of A-Group Graves in Cemetery W — Cont.

	FIGURE	PLATE
W 73 Late		
W 74 no record		
W 75-85 Loci of various dates later than A-Group		

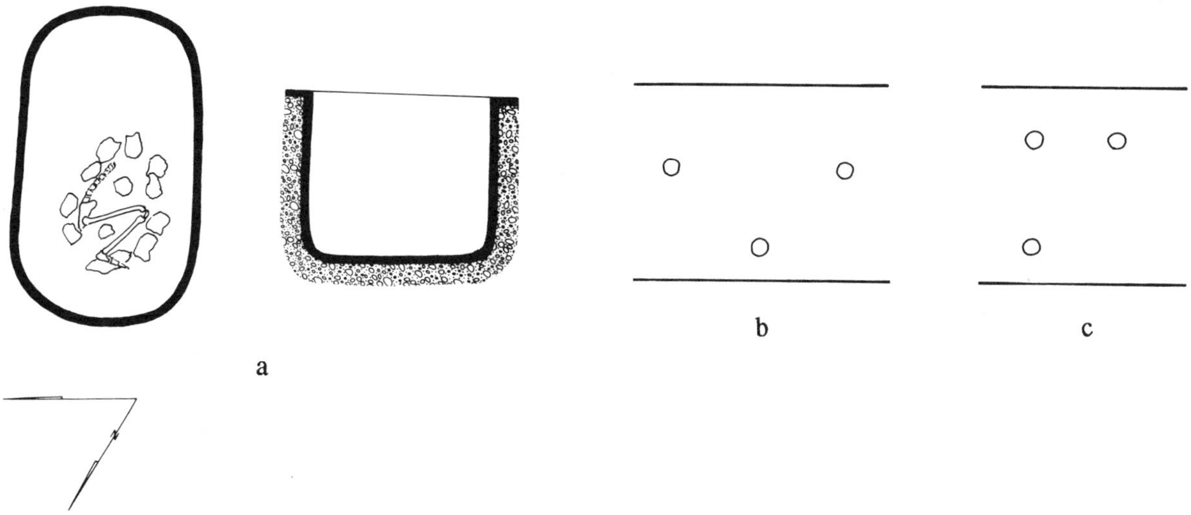

Figure 44. W 72: (a) Plan and section; (b) Position of beam ends in north wall; (c) Position of beam ends in south wall. Scale 1:50.

Table 18—Register of A-Group Graves in Cemetery W — Cont.

	FIGURE	PLATE
W 86 A-Group (?)		
Shaft: circular, 1.56 × 1.63 × .83 m		50a
Burial: —/L/5(?)/d disturbed		
Body: 12-13 years, female		
Objects from shaft:		
1. Bowl	23564	
W 87-88 Late		

V CEMETERIES

Cemeteries VD, VF, VG, and VH were not as closely related to one another as were W1 and W2 (table 19). They consisted of several areas with isolated plots and clusters of graves on the terrace scattered between the houses of Qustul from just below the 125 almost to the 130 contour, distributed over a one kilometer stretch of the village. V 65 and V 67 were the most important A-Group tombs in the cemeteries.

V 78 and V 84 in the center of VF (see pl. 4) may actually have been reused or have been originally made for later burials. VD, actually three small clusters, contained two isolated groups of deposit holes.

VD contained two groups of cache pits, one consisting of V 51 and V 52, and the other consisting of V 57, V 58, and an unnumbered pit. VG (pl. 5) also contained a small group of three circular pits, and seven circular holes were found in VH, but only two were assigned numbers. These had been recut or reshaped for later burials. Sheets of A-Group tombs from VD-G were dated between 20 March and 7 April 1963; VH tombs were excavated on 23 February 1964.

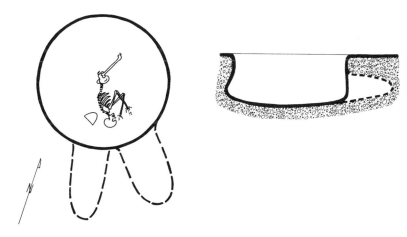

Figure 45. V 51, plan and section. Scale 1:50.

Table 19—Register of A-Group Graves in Cemetery V

			FIGURE	PLATE
V 1-50 Loci of various dates later than A-Group				
V 51 A-Group shaft with later burial (?)			45	
Shaft: circular storage pit, with two narrow extensions				
V 52 A-Group shaft with later burial (?)			46	
Shaft: circular, 1.45 × .35 m			46a	
Burial: E/R/4-5/d				
Body: mature-senile male				
Objects in shaft:				
1. A-Group fine bowl	VI *alpha*-E1b	A 21615	46b	
2. Leather fragments				

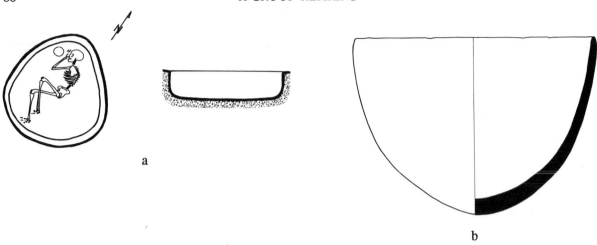

Figure 46. V 52: (a) Plan and section; (b) Bowl, no. 1. Scale (a) 1:50, (b) 2:5.

Table 19—Register of A-Group Graves in Cemetery V — Cont.

	FIGURE	PLATE
V 53-56 New Kingdom and later		
V 57 A-Group shaft with later burial (?)	47	
Shaft: circular, 1.50 × 1.48 × .82 m		
Burial: W/R/5-6/d		
Body: adult-mature		
Objects:		
1. Remains of "loincloth," material uncertain	n/a	
Unnumbered pit near V 57: A-Group (?)	48	
V 58 A-Group shaft with later burial (?)		
Shaft: rect. with rounded ends, 1.57 × .65 × .54 m		
Burial: —		
Objects in shaft:		
1. Jar with lid, 4 pierced lug handles	21720 n/a	

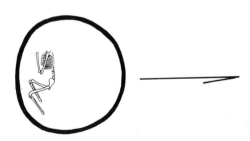

Figure 47. V 57, plan. Scale 1:50.

Figure 48. Unnumbered pit near V 57, plan and section. Scale 1:50

Table 19—Register of A-Group Graves in Cemetery V — Cont.

			FIGURE	PLATE
V 59 A-Group			49-50	
Probably trench and chamber				
Trench: rect. with rounded ends, 5.00 × 1.25 × ca. .62-.87 m			49a	
(Toward the north end is an area of stones beginning				
with a double row across the shaft. Part of the south				
end was cut in the rock.)				
Burial: —				
Body: —				
Objects in shaft:				
1. A-Group Exterior Painted bowl	1-A/38-39	A 24292		17a
Sherds:				18c
I. Exterior Painted:				
A. A/38-39			49e	
B. —/38			49g	
C. A/39 base			49d	
D. A/9			49h	
E. C/27			49b	
F. D/46			49f	
G. —/41			49i	
H. A/39 rim			49d	
I. unc.			49c	
IV. Painted and incised-impressed:				
A. —/2			50a	
VI *alpha*. A-Group fine:				
A. E1			50b	

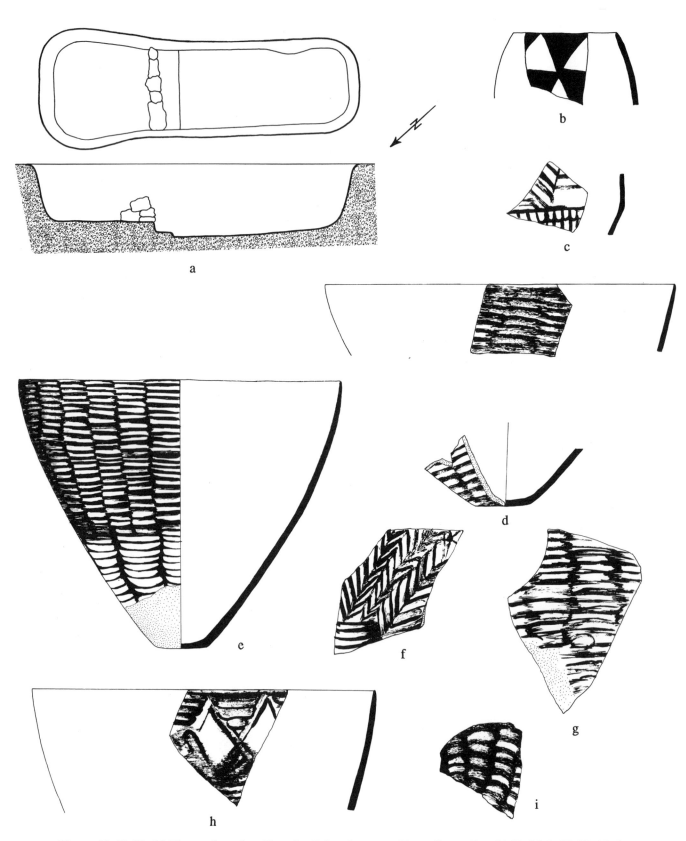

Figure 49. V 59: (a) Plan and section; Exterior Painted pottery, Form Group I— (b) E; (c) I; (d) H; (e) A;
(f) F; (g) B; (h) D; (i) G. Scale 2:5 except (a) 1:50.

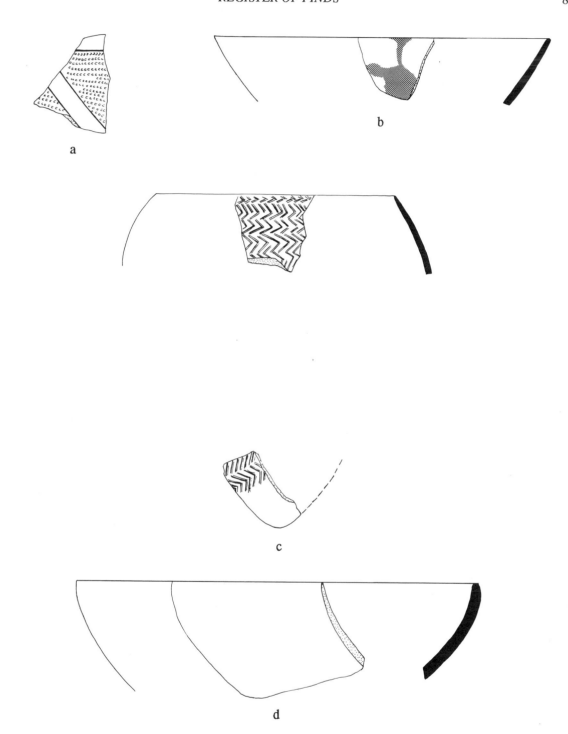

Figure 50. V 59: Pottery— (a) Painted and Incised-Impressed pottery, Form Group IV, A; (b) Simple Fine pottery, Form Group VI *alpha*, A; (c) Sudanese Overall Zone-Incised pottery, Form Group VII, A; (d) Egyptian Hard Pink pottery, Form Group X, A. Scale 2:5.

Table 19—Register of A-Group Graves in Cemetery V — Cont.

	FIGURE	PLATE

V 59   A-Group — Cont.

    VII. Sudanese incised-impressed

        A.   A1 (7.5YR 6/4, some grey)   50c

    X. Egyptian Hard Pink:

        A.   B or E   50d

Note that this seems to have been a tomb with a shaft and side-chamber which was not completely
excavated; the blocking of the chamber was left undisturbed toward the north end.

V 61   Late A-Group, later reused   51

Shaft: rect., 3.78 × 1.26 × .86 m; 4 holes in shaft at N corners

and middle of the sides; remains of stone wall across shaft

between the two sets of holes, probably a secondary partition   51a

Burial: none from A-Group

Body: none from A-Group

Objects from shaft: —

Sherds: 18b

    I. A-Group Exterior Painted:

        A.   A/46   51b

        B.   —/47   51e

        C.   A/41   51c

        D.   —/34   51f

        E.   C/38-39   51d

        F.   C/50   51g

    IV. Painted and incised-impressed:

        A.   A/1   51h

        B.   —/1-2   51i

    VI *alpha*. A-Group fine:

        A.   unc.   51k

    VI *beta*. A-Group miniature:

        A.   A   51j

Note that the partition is not shown.

V 65   Late A-Group, later reused   52

Probably trench and chamber

Trench: rect. with rounded ends, 2.45 × 1.05 × .85 m

    (Depression in surface on SE side indicates presence

    of a collapsed chamber that was not excavated.)   52a

Burial: none from A-Group

Body: none from A-Group

Objects in shaft: —

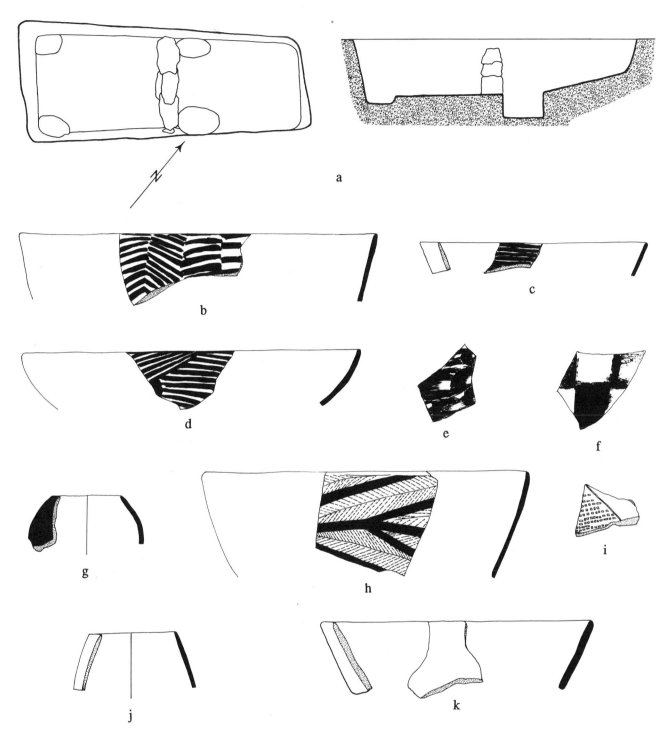

Figure 51. V 61: (a) Plan and section; Pottery—Exterior Painted pottery, Form Group I— (b) A; (c) C; (d) E; (e) B; (f) D; (g) F; Painted and Incised-Impressed pottery, Form Group IV— (h) A; (i) B; (j) Simple Coarse pottery, Form Group VI *beta*, A; (k) Simple Fine pottery, Form Group VI *alpha*, A. Scale 2:5 except (a) 1:50.

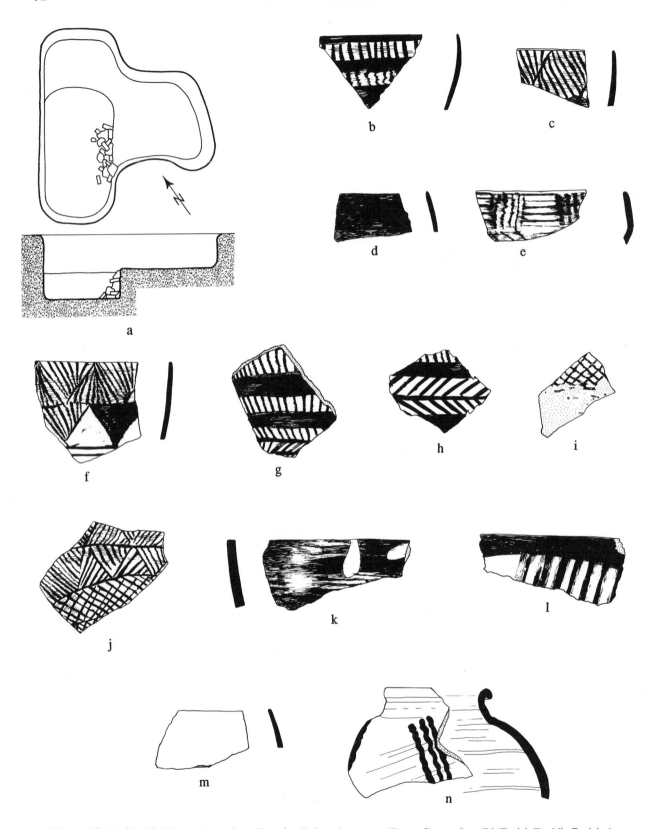

Figure 52. V 65: (a) Plan and section; Exterior Painted pottery, Form Group I— (b) F; (c) B; (d) G; (e) A; (f) D; (g) J; (h) I; (i) C; (j) E; Interior Painted pottery, Form Group V— (k) B; (l) A; (m) Simple Fine pottery, Form Group VI *alpha*, A; (n) Egyptian Hard Pink, Form Group X, A. Scale 2:5 except (a) 1:50.

Table 19—Register of A-Group Graves in Cemetery V — Cont.

				FIGURE	PLATE
V 65 — Cont.					
Sherds:					
I. A-Group Exterior Painted:					18a
A. B/32				52e	
B. A/10				52c	
C. —/5				52i	
D. A/175				52f	
E. E/82				52j	
F. —/57				52b	
G. C/50				52d	
H. B/50?					
I. A/58				52h	
J. A/58— opposed-hatching below				52g	
V. A-Group Interior Painted:					
A. —/7				52l	
B. —/11				52k	
VI *alpha*. A-Group fine:					
A. C2				52m	
X. Egyptian Hard Pink:					
A. AA (lentoid jar, uncertain dimensions)				52n	

V 67 Late A-Group, later reused   53-55

Trench and chamber

Trench: rect., 3.35? × 1.25 × .80 m; step for blocking
ca. 2.50 × .60 × .65 m on SE side   53a

Chamber: 2.75 × 1.20 × 1.50, floor at -1.40 m, roof collapsed

Burial: none from A-Group

Body: none from A-Group

Objects from shaft:

			FIGURE	PLATE
1. 4 bracelets, herringbone dec.; 4 cowrie shells		21886	53e-h	
2. Egyptian bowl	X-F	A 21840	55g	
3. Small bowl		disc.		
4. Copper awl		21885		
5. Cowrie shells		21887		
6. Palette form D with 4 legs	field no. Q2138	Cairo 89864	53b	
7. Palette form D	field no. Q2133	Cairo 89865	53d	
8. Palette form D	field no. Q2135	Cairo 89866	53c	
9. a. Bar of resin/incense and fragments		21884	54a	40
b. 5 polished pebbles				
10. A-Group miniature	VI *beta*-A	A 21839	55c	
(10YR 6/4, grey to black areas on exterior)				

Figure 53. V 67: (a) Plan and section; Palettes— (b) No. 6; (c) No. 8; (d) No. 7; Bracelets— (e-h) No. 1;
(i) Incense burner, no. 17; (j) Mortar, no. 18. Scale 2:5 except (a) 1:50.

Figure 54. V 67 and contents: (a) Mortar and pestle, no. 19; (b) Bar of incense, no. 9a; Pottery—
(c) No. 22; (d) No. 13; (e) No. 16; (f) No. 24; (g) No. 25; (h) No. 26. Scale 2:5.

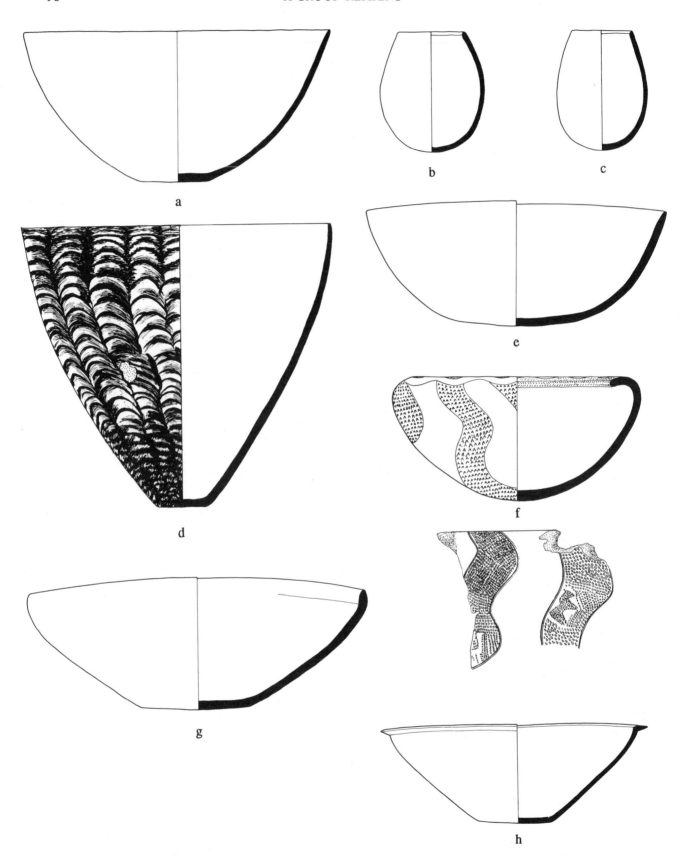

Figure 55. V 67: Pottery— (a) No. 14; (b) No. 11; (c) No. 10; (d) No. 15; (e) No. 12; (f) No. 23; (g) No. 2; (h) No. 21. Scale 2:5 except (h) 1:5.

Table 19—Register of A-Group Graves in Cemetery V — Cont.

			FIGURE	PLATE
V 67 — Cont.				
Objects from shaft:				
11. A-Group miniature (burn.)	VI *beta*-A	B 21872	55b	
12. A-Group fine bowl, red	VI *alpha*-E3b	A 21873	55e	
13. A-Group Exterior Painted bowl	I-A/55	A 21875	54d	
14. A-Group fine bowl (burn. D)	VI *alpha*-B2	B 21874	55a	
15. A-Group Exterior Painted bowl	I-A/46	B 21877	55d	16a
16. A-Group Exterior Painted cup (2.5YR 3/6, 7.5YR 7/4)	I-C/121	C 21879	54e	
17. Incense burner		21880	53j	
18. Mortar form C		21881	53i	
19. Mortar form A and pestle		21882	54a	
20. Pebbles		21884		
21. Egyptian bowl	X-M2	B 21965	55h	
22. A-Group Exterior Painted bowl	I-B/48	D 21966	54c	16e
23. Heavy incised bowl (7.5 YR 5/4 to neutral grey)	VIII-12	A 21967	55f	34-35
24. A-Group Exterior Painted bowl (2.5YR 4/6 5YR 6/4)	I-A/141-142	E 21968	54f	
25. A-Group Exterior Painted bowl	I-A/47	F 21969	54g	
26. A-Group Exterior Painted bowl	I-B/141-142	G 21970	54h	

Sherds:

A-Group Exterior Painted:

    H. A/38

    I. A/40-41

    J. —/49

    K. —/38-45

    L. C/50

V 78 A-Group?

Shaft: circular, .70 (opening) - .84 (bottom) × 1.00 m   56

Burial: L/S/3/d

Body: "Infant II," female

Objects: —

V 84 A-Group? or probably later.

Shaft: irregular pit, 1.40 × 1.10 × .76 m

Burial: intrusive, later

Body: —

Objects: —

Table 19—Register of A-Group Graves in Cemetery V — Cont.

	FIGURE	PLATE

V 85 A-Group pit, later intrusive burial
    Shaft: A. 1.44 × 1.42 × .41 m, circular
                  B. elongated area at N end of pit ca. 1.42 m with extended burial

Figure 56. V 78, plan and section. Scale 1:50.

CEMETERY S

Cemetery S (table 20) included two small clusters of loci, located directly south of VA, somewhat below the 125 contour (5). Four shafts were dug toward the south end of the area in the Late A-Group and later plundered; S 3 was reused in the New Kingdom. The shapes of the shafts were unusual; for example, three were rectangular. S 3 contained a roughly hewn stone slab that may have been a stela. It seems likely that these shafts were part of the Cemetery L complexes, possibly associated with valley enclosures of the kind shown on the incense burners.[42] The four were evidently not tombs because no bones were found. The grave sheets were dated 10-11 March 1963.

Table 20—Register of A-Group Graves in Cemetery S

		FIGURE	PLATE
S 1	A-Group deposit pit	57	
	Shaft: oval pit .80 × .60 × .40 m	57a	
	Objects from shaft:		
	1. Three carnelian pendants	21380 n/a	
	2. Six shell bracelets	21381 57b	
	3. Ostrich eggshell fragments	21382	
	4. Alabaster cup or miniature jar	21383 57c	37e

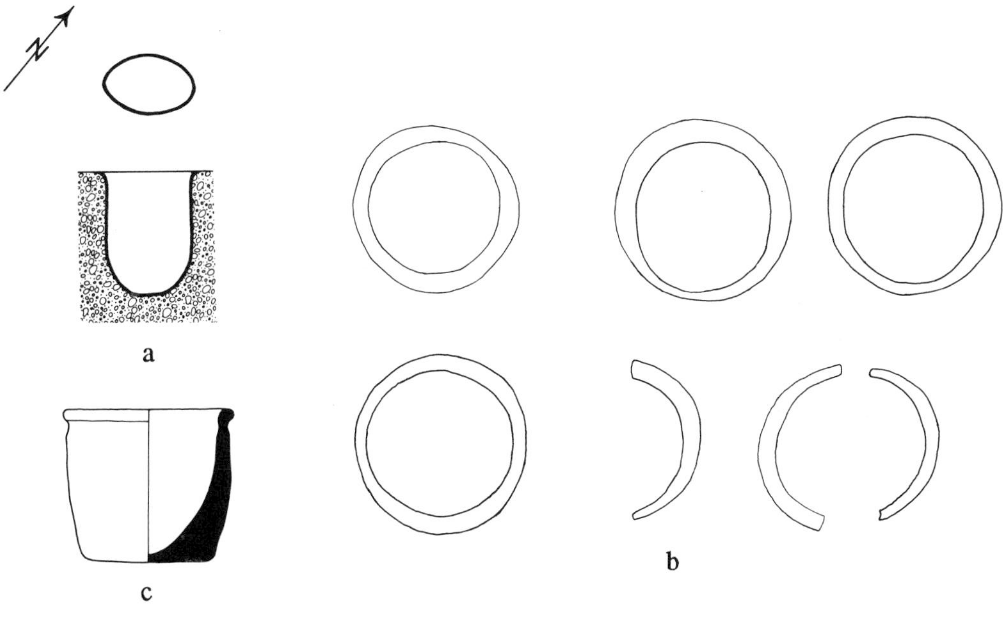

Figure 57. S 1: (a) Plan and section; (b) Bracelets, no. 2; (c) Stone vessel, no. 4. Scale 2:5 except (a) 1:50.

Table 20—Register of A-Group Graves in Cemetery S — Cont.

				FIGURE	PLATE
S 2	Late A-Group deposit pit			58	
	Shaft: rect., one end rounded, other with rounded corners,			58a	
	2.05 × .80 × .40 m				
	Objects in shaft:				
	1. Mortar form A		21255	58b	
	2. Pebbles		21256		
	3. Ivory rings, 2, one complete, one fragment		21385		
	Sherds:				
	I. A-Group Exterior Painted				
	A. A/4	4 sherds		58e	
	B. A/10	1 sherds		58f	
	C. A?/10	2 sherds			
	D. A?/23	1 sherds		58d	
	E. A?/23	1 sherds			
	F. A/27	1 sherds		58c	
	G. unc. combination of 119 and 32, 1 sherd				
S 3	Late A-Group deposit pit (reused later)				
	Shaft: 2.85 × .90-.95 × 1.10 m; round depression in center, .35 × .20 m			59a	
	Burial: none from A-Group				
	Body: none from A-Group				
	Objects of A-Group deposit in shaft:				
	1. A-Group miniature	VI *beta*-A	A 21414	59j	
	2. A-Group miniature	VI *beta*-A	B 21415	59k	
	3. A-Group miniature (other shape) VI *beta*-C		C 21416	59h	
	4. Palette form D		21407A	59d	
	5. Palette form C		21407B	59e	
	6. Ivory pin with decorated head		21406A	59b	42a, 43c
	7. Ivory jar		21406B	59c	42b, 43b
	8. Fragment of ivory jar		21406C		43a
	9. A-Group Exterior Painted bowl I-F/176		F sherds	59f	
	10. Large jar		disc.		
	11. Stela		disc.	60d	

Figure 58. S 2: (a) Plan and section; (b) Mortar, no. 1; Exterior Painted pottery, Form Group I— (c) F; (d) D; (e) A; (f) B. Scale 2:5 except (a) 1:50.

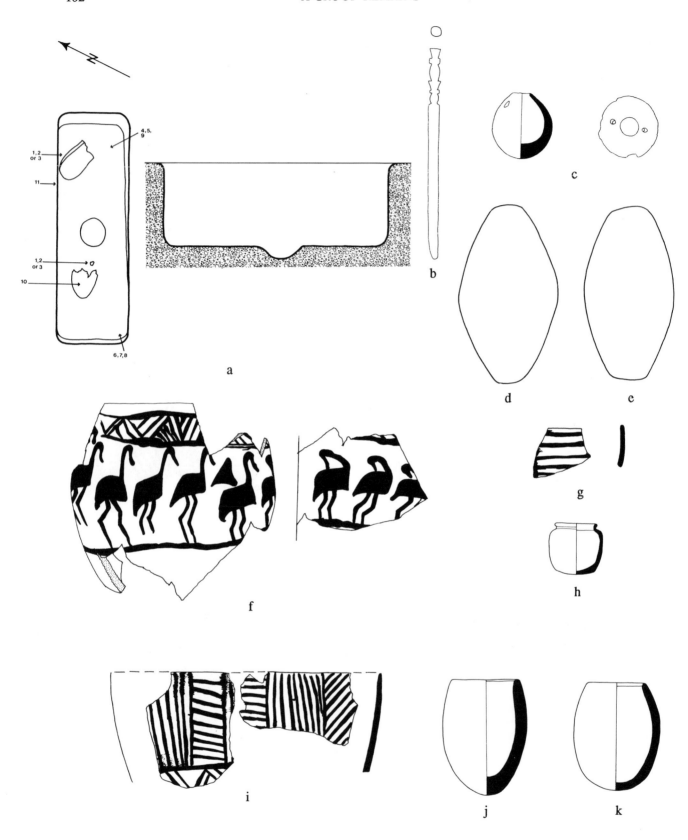

Figure 59. S 3: (a) Plan and section; (b) Ivory pin, no. 6; (c) Ivory vessel, no. 7; Palettes— (d) No. 4; (e) No. 5; Pottery— (f) No. 9; (g) Exterior Painted pottery, Form Group I, C; (h) No. 3; (i) Exterior Painted pottery, Form Group I, A; (j) No. 1; (k) No. 2. Scale 2:5 except (a) 1:50.

Table 20—Register of A-Group Graves in Cemetery S — Cont.

			FIGURE	PLATE
S 3 — Cont.				
Sherds:				
I. A-Group Exterior Painted				17c
A. A/81b	3 sherds		59i	
B. A/38	1			
C. C/38	1		59g	
D. A?/23	1			
E. A?/23	1			
F. F/176 bowl			59f	
S 4 A-Group deposit pit			60	
Shaft: rect. with rounded corners, 2.75 × 1.05 × .85 m			60a	
Objects in shaft:				
1. Incense burner		21254	60c	
2. Ostrich eggshell, almost complete		21384		
(few fragments missing, hole in end, 2.1 × 1.5 cm)				
Sherd:				
I. A-Group Exterior Painted				
A. ?/39			60b	17c

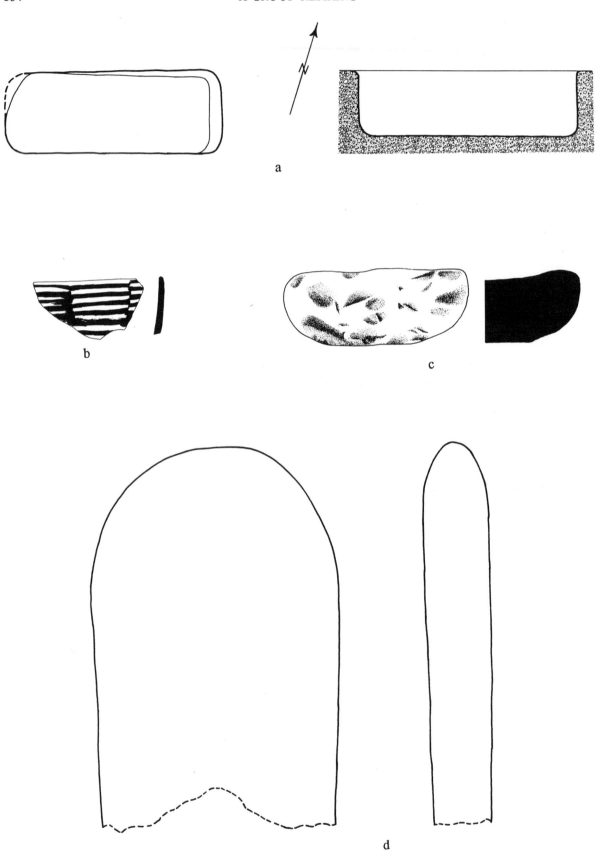

Figure 60. S 4: (a) Plan and section; (b) Sherd, Form Group I, A; (c) Incense burner, no. 1; S 3:
(d) Reconstruction of a stela, no. 11. Scale (a) 1:50, (b), (c) 2:5, (d) ca. 1:5.

CEMETERY Q

Various parts of Cemetery Q (pls. 6-7, Emery and Kirwan's 220), the X-Group royal cemetery at Qustul, had been used earlier, during the A-Group and Meroitic periods. As is the case with most of the other cemeteries, Q straddled the 125 m contour and was bisected by a shallow *khor*. No tombs were dug in the area during the A-Group period, but various small groups of cache pits were discovered (table 21). When the area was reused for burials in the Meroitic, X-Group, and Christian periods, a few of these pits were reused and even recut to accommodate later burials. In addition, some new circular pits were made in X-Group times. These were generally wide and shallow depressions which are easily distinguished from A-Group cache pits.

Four areas contained pits that were probably A-Group in origin. A. The southernmost, near the southwest corner of Q (pl. 6), however, is the least certain. It consists of four empty circular pits identified by the numbered X-Group tombs nearby. Since none of them contained objects, they are identified only by their shape. B. Cache pit Q 80, which contained three sealed A-Group pots with domestic objects (pl. 7), was found alone near the southern end of the northern half of Cemetery Q. C. A small group of four pits was found in the northwest corner of the cemetery (pl. 7). D. Twelve A-Group pits were found in the area northeast of Tumulus 48 (pl. 7), which was later occupied by the Meroitic cemetery. Q 631 contained five inverted jars.

The following numbered circular pits contained no objects that would determine dates and might well be A-Group: Q 241, Q 457, Q 611, Q 615, Q 616, Q 656, Q 657, Q 662, Q 671, Q 672, and Q 673 (near Q 681 and cut by Q 571). The unnumbered circular pits found near Q 2, Q 3, Q 6, and Q 9 in the southern sector might also be A-Group. Many other pits were found which were probably X-Group.

Cemetery Q was excavated through the 1962-63 season, and the burial sheets of A-Group pits were dated from 13 December 1962 to 10 April 1964.

Table 21—Register of A-Group Graves in Cemetery Q

					FIGURE	PLATE
Q 80	Middle A-Group storage pit				61-62	55
	Shaft: circular, 1.20 × 1.20 m, depression in center, .40 × .30 m					
	(The depression may have marked the opening of a second					
	chamber at a lower level which was not excavated.)				61a	
	Objects in shaft:					
	1. A-Group coarse jar, sealing	VI *gamma*-F	A 20160		61d, 62b	
	2. Egyptian narrow jar, sealing	X-W	A 20161		61c, 62a	
	3. Pestle from 1		20262A		61e	
	4. Oval pestle from 1		20262B		61f	
	5. Natural (?), pebble roughened and used as palette, malachite		20262C		61h	
	6. Natural (?), pebble roughened on one side and used as a palette, with black discoloration		20262D		61g	

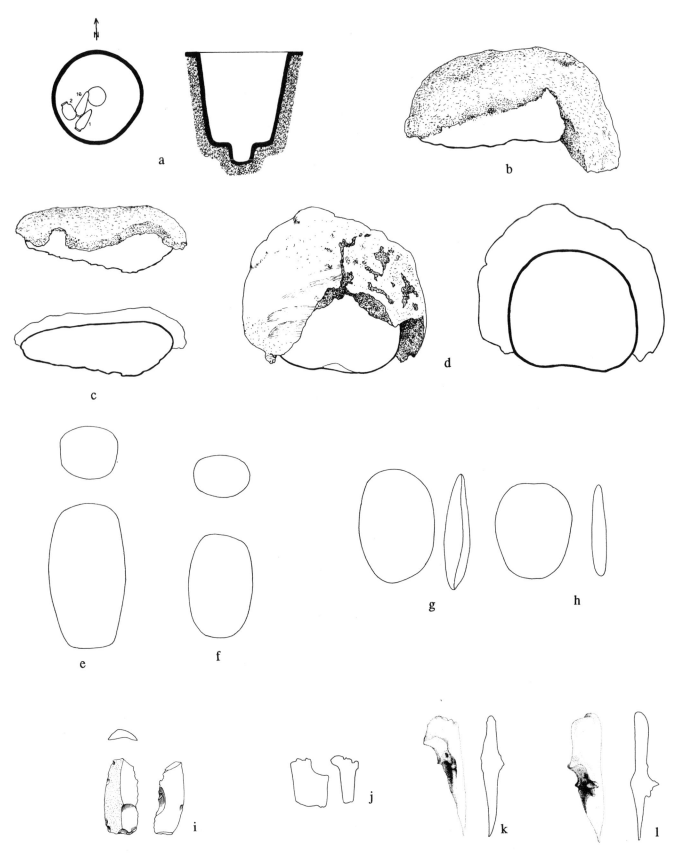

Figure 61. Q 80 and contents: (a) Plan and section; (b) Sealing from jar no. 16; (c) Sealing from jar no. 2; (d) Sealing from jar no. 1; Palettes— (e) No. 3; (f) No. 4; (g) No. 6; (h) No. 5; (i) Flint blade, no. 7; Bone tools— (j) No. 11; (k) No. 8; (l) No. 9. Scale 2:5 except (a) 1:50.

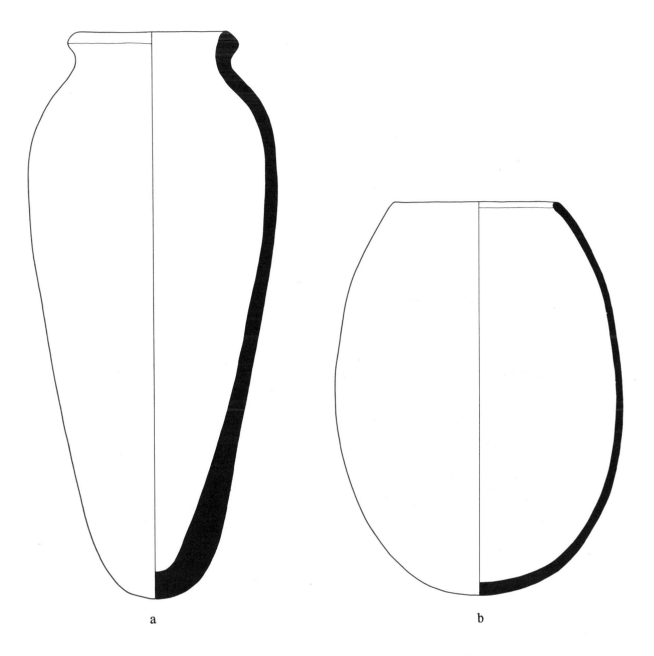

Figure 62. Q 80, pottery: (a) No. 2; (b) No. 1. Scale 2:5.

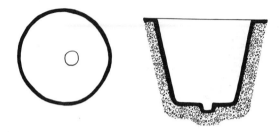

Figure 63. Q 611 plan and section. Scale 1:50.

Table 21—Register of A-Group Graves in Cemetery Q — Cont.

		FIGURE	PLATE
Q 80 — Cont.			
7. Flint blade with coarse denticulation, signs of wear and cortex	20262E	61i	
8. Bone awl	20262F	61k	
9. Bone awl	20262G	61l	
10. Polished green pebble	20262H		
11. Fragment of bone awl	20262I	61j	
12. Flint flake	20306A		
13. Fragment, ochre-bearing stone	20306B		
14. Fragments, malachite	20306C		
15. Leather fragments, one tied as if neck of bag, used to contain 20306 A-C ?	20306D		
16. Egyptian narrow jar, sealing, X-W sealing	jar disc. 20181C	61b	

Note that objects 5-11 were contained in number 2; objects 3-4 and 12-15 were in number 1.

Cemetery Q, northern sector, A-Group, northwest angle:

Q 288 A-Group
    Shaft: circular, plastered with mud, small hole in the side near bottom,
        reused late; dimensions 1.70 × 1.10 m

Near Q 288 A-Group?
    Shaft: circular, dimensions unknown

Q 289 A-Group? reused at uncertain date
    Shaft: irregular, probably originally circular

Q 457 A-Group? reused late
    Shaft: circular, 1.50 × .80 m

Cemetery Q, northern sector, A-Group, northeast area:

Q 611 A-Group
    Shaft: circular, 1.10 × 1.10 m

Table 21—Register of A-Group Graves in Cemetery Q — Cont

			FIGURE	PLATE

Q 615 A-Group
    Shaft: circular, $1.00 \times .95$ m

Q 616 A-Group
    Shaft: circular, 1.10×1.15 m

Q 631 A-Group (Middle?) storage pit   64-65   50b
    Shaft: circular, no dimensions given, described as denuded   64a
    Objects in shaft, placed upside down on a layer of sand in the bottom:

				FIGURE	PLATE
1. A-Group rippled jar	II-G	A	21898	64b	20a
2. A-Group rippled jar	II-H	B	21899	64c	20b
3. A-Group rippled jar	II-I	C	21900	65b	20d
4. A-Group rippled jar	II-J	D	21901	65a	20c
5. A-Group jar, rippled?			disc.		

Q 632 A-Group storage pit, Middle?
    Shaft: circular, no dimensions given
    Objects in shaft: —
    Sherds:
        A. A-Group rippled   n/a
        B. "other sherd"   n/a

Q 656 A-Group
    Shaft: circular, $.90 \times .90$ m

Q 657 A-Group
    Shaft: circular, $1.00 \times .95$ m

Q 662 A-Group
    Shaft: circular, $1.00 \times .95$ m

Q 671 A-Group
    Shaft: circular, $.60 \times .50$ m

Q 672 A-Group   66
    Shaft: circular, $.93 \times .60$ m

Near Q 681 A-Group
    Shaft: circular, $.90 \times .70$ m

Cut by Q 571 A-Group ?
    Shaft: circular, dimensions unknown

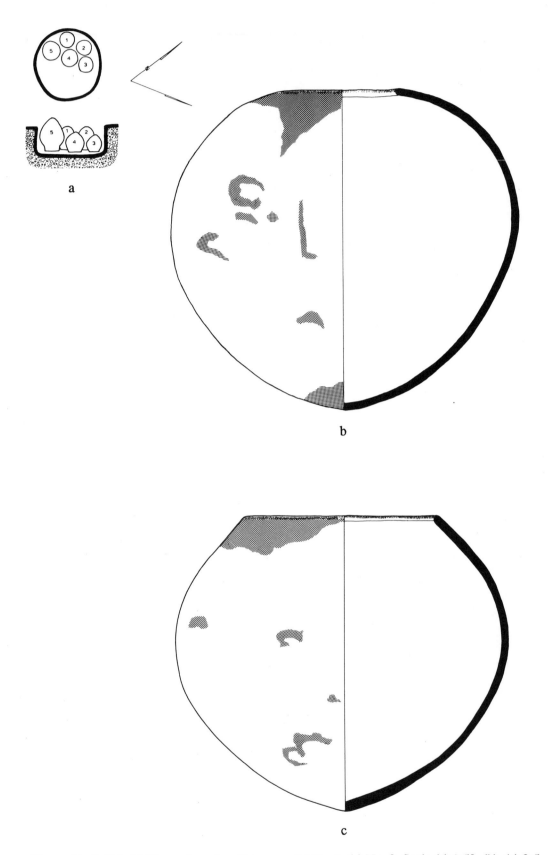

Figure 64. Q 631: (a) Plan and section; Pottery— (b) No. 1; (c) No. 2. Scale (a) 1:50, (b), (c) 2:5.

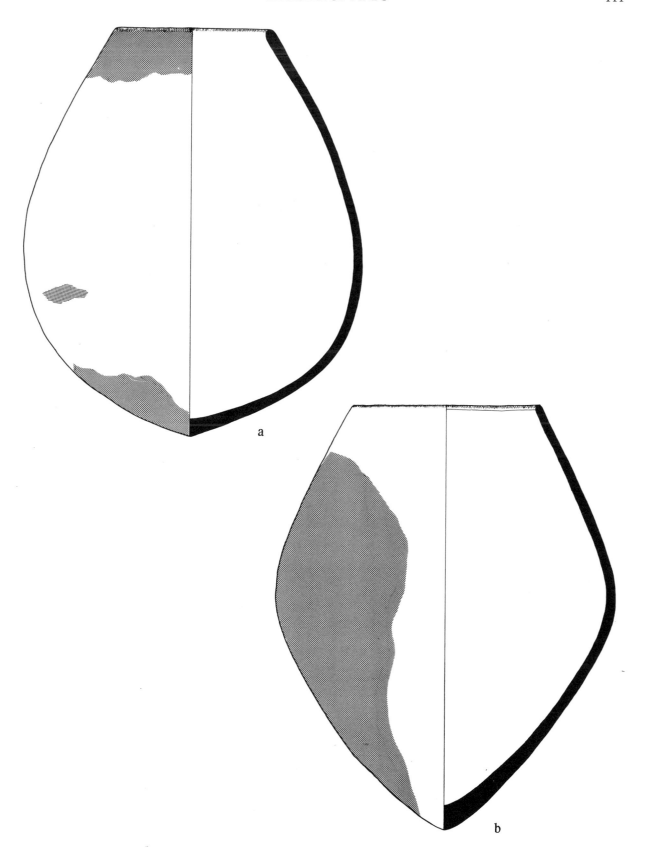

Figure 65. Q 631, pottery: (a) No. 4; (b) No. 3. Scale 2:5.

Figure 66. Q 672, plan and section. Scale 1:50.

CEMETERY T

Like the pits in Cemetery Q, the A-Group and post-A-Group tombs of Cemetery T were scattered among the tombs of a large later cemetery (table 22).[43] Grave sheets were dated from 13 January to 2 February 1964.

Table 22—Register of A-Group Graves in Cemetery T

			FIGURE	PLATE
T 75 A-Group				
Shaft: rect. with rounded corners (SW-NE), 1.84 × .92 × .57-.76 m				
Max. depth at SW end of pit			67a	
Burials: A. —				
B. —				
Bodies: A. Mature female				
B. 6 1/2- 7 1/2 years				
Objects from shaft:				
1. Egyptian jar	X-AB	A 23219.	67b	
2. Beads: gn. fai. balls, irreg. 6 × 5.5 mm 2		samp.	67d	37i
T 110 A-Group				
Shaft: .70 × .35 × .40 m (child burial)				
Burial: in jar, head SW				
Body: 2-3 years				
Objects in shaft:				
1. Egyptian jar used for burial	X-W	A 24168	67c	
2. Egyptian small jar	X-R2	B 23273		
T 113 A-Group				
Shaft: no information available				
Burial: same				
Body: same				
Objects from shaft:				
1. Egyptian wavy-handled jar	X-P	A 24254	68	
2. Egyptian coarse jar	XI-B	A sherds		
3. Egyptian coarse jar	XI-B	B sherds		
4. Beads		samp. n/a		
T 128 A-Group			69	
Shaft: rect. with rounded corners, 1.10 × .60 × .70 m			69a	
Burial: —				
Body: adult male				

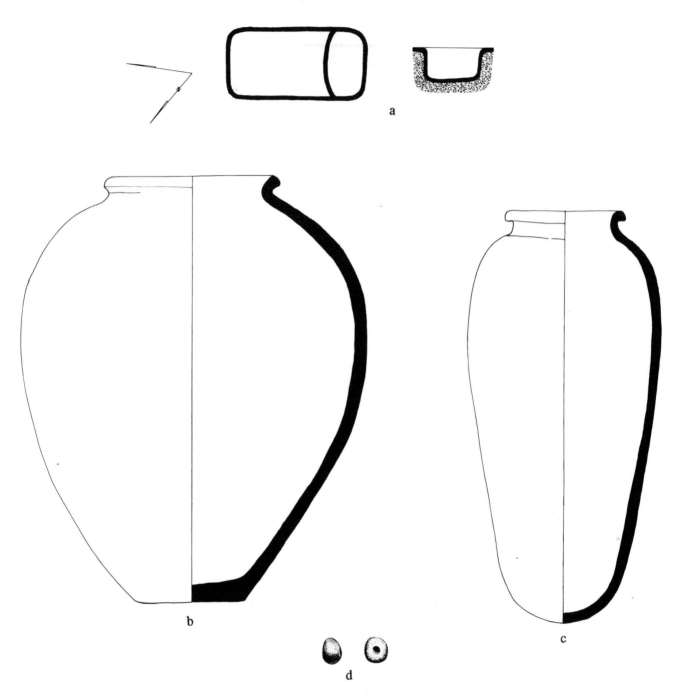

Figure 67. T 75 and T 110: (a) T 75, plan and section; (b) Jar, T 75—1; (c) Jar, T 110—1; (d) Bead, T 75—2. Scale (a) 1:50, (b) 2:5, (c) 1:5, (d) 4:5.

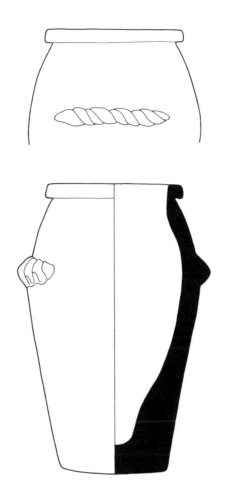

Figure 68. Jar, T 113—1. Scale 2:5.

Table 22—Register of A-Group Graves in Cemetery T — Cont.

			FIGURE	PLATE
T 128 — Cont.				
Objects from shaft:				
1. Egyptian coarse jar	XI-B	A 23195	69c	
2. Coarse incised pointed jar	XI ?	B sherds n/a		
3. Egyptian bowl (sherd)	X-F	A sherds	69b	

T 153 A-Group?

Shaft:	A.	1.10 × .90 × .60 m
	B.	1.30 × 1.00 × .83 m
Burials:	A.	—
	B.	S/1/—/—
Bodies:	A.	Adult, male?
	B.	Adult, female?

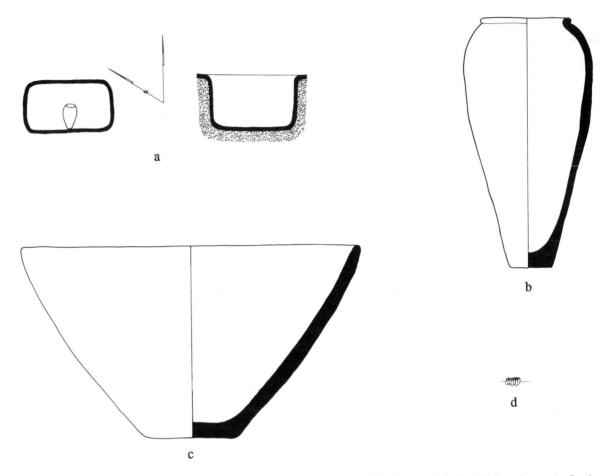

Figure 69. T 128: (a) Plan and section; Pottery— (b) No. 3; (c) No. 1; T 243: (d) Bead, no. 1. Scale (a) 1:50, (b) 2:5, (c) 1:5, (d) 4:5.

Table 22—Register of A-Group Graves in Cemetery T — Cont.

		FIGURE	PLATE
T 243 A-Group or possibly later			
Shaft: .80 × .45 × .20 m (NE-SW)			
Burial: N/R/5/c?			
Body: 6 1/2- 7 1/2 years			
Objects in shaft:			
1. Beads:	samp.	69d	37p
dk. gn. fai. discs, 13			
ca. 2-2.5 × 1-1.5 mm (two groups strung, 3 and 5 beads each)			

Table 22—Register of A-Group Graves in Cemetery T — Cont.

FIGURE   PLATE

Possible later tombs in Cemetery T

T 11   A-Group?

Shaft: oval, $1.00 \times .58 \times .63$ m

Burial: —

Body: child

Objects from shaft:

    1. Beads   21532

        a. car. baggy   1

        b. end, gast. shell   1

        c. irreg. dio. size 3   1

        d. blue fai. bar,   5

            $3-4 \times 2-3$ mm

        e. bl. fai. size 1   13

        f. dark blue-gn. fai. size 1   163

        g. ost. egg size 1   131

Note that the baggy carnelian bead from T 11 is A-Group; the dull dark green or blue faience beads from T 243 and T 11 are the same as those from T 155.

T 247 A-Group?

Shaft: rect. with rounded ends, $1.00 \times .55 \times .75$ m

Burial: S/L/6-7/e

Body: 6 1/2 years

Objects:

    1. Beads   samp.

        a. irreg. unfinished   1

            dio. size 3+

        b. dull fai., size 2   3

        c. gn. gl. size 1   1

NOTES

1. *OINE* III, p. 14, table 4.

2. For a more detailed discussion of the various kinds of tombs and their occurrence, see *OINE* III, pp. 14–18. For a scheme of classes of important burials in Egypt, see Kaiser and Dreyer 1982, pp. 242–53.

3. This kind of tomb was also found in Sudan by the Scandinavian Joint Expedition (Nordström 1972, pl. 65, 298:4). It is very important here as a link between the burial customs of A-Group and those of Kerma (*OINE* III, pp. 183–84; Bietak 1968, p. 125, K 5).

4. The widespread occurrence of such pits away from settlements is discussed in Williams 1982.

5. See *OINE* IX (forthcoming), chapter 1. Many of the X-Group pits were broad, shallow depresssions lined with mud; they often contained X-Group pottery.

6. *OINE* III, pp. 14–18.

7. *OINE* III, pp. 21–26 and figs. 2–4. For a general discussion of classification, see pp. 191–95.

8. *OINE* III, pp. 27–29, and pp. 31–60, table 9.

9. Colors are presented according to the Munsell Soil Color Chart (1975 edition) except for grey and black. Colors were not presented in this way in *OINE* III because so many vessels were discolored. The colors of Syro-Palestinian type jugs, Form Group XII, are added here to complete the representation of colors for all of the groups. L24 XII-A has a pale brown or greyish exterior 10YR 7/4, with light red areas 2.5YR 6/6 and some greyish areas 10YR 6/1. The interior is black. L 24 XII-B is light red, 2.5YR 6/6, varying slightly to light brown, 10 YR 7/2. C is 2.5YR 5/6 to 2.5YR 6/6, a slightly variable surface. Brown-coated vessel D is 2.5YR 4/4 on a ground color 2.5YR 6/6, while the coat of E is 2.5YR 4/6.

10. *OINE* III, p. 30. This Form Group was not subdivided in *OINE* III because it was rare in Cemetery L.

11. Nordström 1972, pls. 44 and 45.

12. *OINE* III, p. 61, and table 11.

13. See p. 41 below.

14. See *OINE* III, figs. 22b and 26a and pp. 153–56. See also Williams 1988, p. 15 and fig. 6. It is cited there as W 6–8; a detailed review of the tomb list and register confirm that it is W 11–8.

15. *OINE* III, pp. 61–62, and pp. 74–75, tables 13–14. A few fragments from unusual shapes were found in Cemetery L.

16. *OINE* III, p. 62, and p. 79, table 15. Miniatures in Cemetery L were all of form A, and therefore the group was not subdivided.

17. Eiwanger 1984, p. 27. Williams (*OINE* V, p. 40) attributed the effect to wiping, but Eiwanger showed that it was due to scraping with a fresh-water mollusc shell.

18. *OINE* III, p. 62 and p. 80, table 16.

19. *OINE* III, pp. 62–63 and p. 82, table 17.

20. *OINE* III, pp. 63–65 and p. 84, table 18. For the deeply impressed decoration found on many of these vessels from the Shendi area, see Geus and Reinold 1979, pl. XXXIII.

21. *OINE* III, pp. 67–74 and pp. 86–90, table 19. A comparable jar with lugs and a very elaborately painted palm tree made up of of wavy lines was found at Ashkeit (Nordström 1972, pls. 47: 8 and 79: 308:56–2). These vessels show that the pots with three vertical lugs continue into Naqada III. See p. 41 below and Williams 1988, pp. 13–14.

22. *OINE* III, pp. 76–78 and pp. 99–100, table 20.

23. *OINE* III, p. 131.

24. *OINE* III, pp. 108–12; see especially table 25.

25. *OINE* III, pp. 112–14.

26. *OINE* III, pp. 114–15.

27. The complete absence of shell hooks and tokens is particularly noteworthy considering the proximity of Cemetery L.

28. For pebbles with palettes, see *OINE* III, p. 116, table 30.

29. *OINE* III, p. 128; Petrie 1920, pl. VIII: 15.

30. For ivory vessels, see Petrie 1920, pl. XLVIII and Baumgartel 1960, pp. 57–58. Although a few round-based vessels were found in Badarian contexts (Brunton and Caton-Thompson 1928, pl. XXIII: 1, 2, 4, and 9), none closely resembles the vessels from Cemeteries L and S. For other ivory vessels in A-Group, see Hofmann 1967, p. 107.

31. *OINE* III, pp. 130–31. For an oval cake of resin, see Reisner 1910, p. 20, fig. 1, Cemetery 7.104.9.

32. For metal tools and weapons in A-Group, see Nordström 1972, p. 123–24, and Hofmann 1967, pp. 105–6.

33. Nordström 1972, pl. 55.

34. For a discussion of the Faras Seal, see *OINE* III, pp. 167–68. See also Björkman and Säve-Söderbergh 1972, for a discussion of this composition.

35. *OINE* III, pp. 169–71.

36. Björkman and Säve-Söderbergh cited parallels from Egypt and, ultimately, Mesopotamia. See Williams and Logan 1987, for the place this composition occupies in a cycle of Egyptian themes.

37. *OINE* III, pl. 81c and table 40, IIB8. The granary mark also occurred in the Sudanese area (Nordström 1972, pl. 26, 13.332/53A:13).

In *OINE* III, table 40, pp. 148–49, the potmarks in the list were intended to accompany small illustrations that would serve as a guide to the corpus (pls. 76–83). Unfortunately, when the volume was in page proofs, this proved not to be feasible and the citations in the table were made much less direct than is desirable. Note that table 40 is intended to be a guide to the marks rather than a complete register list, and there were some fragmentary and doubtful marks that were not classified in it. For IA1, see *OINE* III, pl. 81b; for IA2, see pl. 81f; for IA3, see pl. 82h (above right); for IA4, see pl. 79m; for IA5, see pl. 78c; for IA6, see pl. 79g; for IA7, see pl. 83a; for IA8, see pl. 78h, right; for IA9, see pl. 78g; for IA10, see pl. 79j; for IA11, see pl. 81m, right (pl. 79f may be the same, doubled); for IA12, see pls. 81e and 82j (slightly different versions); for IA13, see pl. 79d (above). For IB1, see pl. 80d (pendant lines); for IB2, see pl. 81r (note that the example in the list is not illustrated); for IB3, see pl. 81g; for IB4, see pl. 79n; for IB5, see pl. 78e; for IB6, see pl. 81k. For IC1, see pls. 78j, 79a, and 83b (below); for IC2, see pl 78h; for IC3, see pl. 78d; for IC4, see pl. 79o (the figure could also be a catfish); for IC5, see pl. 78f; for IC6, see pl. 79c, h, and possibly pl. 76, above left, the incomplete sign in the main inscription; IC7 is cited. For IIA1, see pl. 76; for IIA2, see pl.80a; for IIA3, see pl. 80b; for IIA4, see pl. 80c, d (except for pendant lines); for IIA5, see pls. 96a and 97. For IIB1, see pl. 79k; for IIB2, see pl. 83b above; for IIB3, see pl. 76, above center; for IIB4, see pl. 76, lower left; for IIB5, see pl. 78a; for IIB6, see pl. 81a; for IIB7, see pl. 79i; for IIB8, see pls. 81c, q, and 82; for IIB9, see pl. 81i and m; for IIB10, see pls. 79e and l; for IIB11, see pl. 78b.

The nested meander probably had some meaning, but it is difficult to assign it to any of the larger classes. In addition, as pointed out above, a number of marks in Cemetery L, such as pls. 78k, 79b, 80e, 81d, and 81j, are not classified. Some, such as pls. 78k and 81j, may be trees.

38. *OINE* III, pp. 147–150. The elaborate closed or nested meander did not occur in Cemetery L.

39. Petrie 1921, pl. XXXIV: 45b, S; XXXV: 50, 50B, 51M; Petrie and Quibell, 1896, pl. XXXIV: 45, 56b, 57, 58.

40. For a detailed discussion of the palm in early art, see Williams 1988, especially pp. 7–16. See also note 21 above and *OINE* III, pp. 152–54.

41. The relation between serpents and the palm tree is discussed in Williams 1988 generally. See also *OINE* III, pp. 152–56.

42. See below, pp. 137–39, Section C of Chapter 4.

43. For details of Cemetery T, see *OINE* V, pp. 1–23.

3

EXCAVATIONS BETWEEN ABU SIMBEL AND THE SUDAN FRONTIER
KEITH C. SEELE, DIRECTOR. PART 4:

POST-A-GROUP REMAINS AT ADINDAN

One of the archaeological problems that has been considered solved in recent years has been that of the so-called B-Group in Lower Nubia.[1] Some time ago, H. S. Smith pointed out that materials had been assigned to the period of the Old Kingdom based on vague or inconsistent criteria. Reisner originally established the B-Group using features that also appear in materials assigned to the A- or C-Group phases.[2] His group included many merely poor graves.[3] Later, Firth used criteria different from Reisner's to assign tombs to the B-Group.[4] Because the B-Group could not be clearly distinguished from the A- or C-Groups using Reisner and Firth's criteria, Smith's work has promoted its elimination as an archaeological phase.[5] Instead of occupation by a distinct B-Group, he concluded that Lower Nubia in the Old Kingdom was occupied only by Egyptians and possibly a few local inhabitants whose poor remains are indistinguishable from those of earlier and later times.[6] In addition, Smith showed that the end of A-Group dated to the early First Dynasty rather than the end of the Archaic period, as Reisner had proposed. The higher date for the end of A-Group and the abolition of B-Group left a long period between the First and the Sixth Dynasties during which Lower Nubia was depopulated.[7] This hiatus ended with the C-Group's repopulation of the area and the appearance of several major political entities south of Aswan during the Sixth Dynasty.[8] This gap would then parallel a later hiatus widely recognized in the literature on Nubia which dates to the period extending from the late New Kingdom to the end of the first millennium B.C.[9] Although Smith's discussion was based on a clear statement of the problem in two questions, "Is the B-Group a cultural group, distinct from all other cultural groups? If so, what date should it be assigned?,"[10] it did not deal completely with the problem of Old Kingdom (or by now late Archaic and Old Kingdom) materials in Lower Nubia. However, the lack of published details did not permit these questions or questions implied by the first two to be answered. Ever since Smith's study, it has been generally accepted that in Lower Nubia no materials could be dated to the later Archaic and Old Kingdom periods. However, as the examination of materials from Cemetery T proceeded,[11] it became apparent that certain tombs could not be assigned a date in either the A- or C-Groups. It was therefore necessary to ask additional questions to complete Smith's inquiry: "Are there any materials in Lower Nubia which must be dated to the period between the A- and C-Groups or the late Archaic and Old Kingdom periods? If so, do they represent a distinct archaeological group?" Positive answers to these questions would imply still another question: "Which, if any, of the traditional groups found in Lower Nubia does this group resemble?"

A. TWO POST-A-GROUP BURIALS AT ADINDAN

Two tombs in Cemetery T at Adindan were very different from graves that belonged to the A- and C-Groups, T 35 and T 155. The more important of the two, T 155, was originally assumed to be C-Group because stones aligned at the edge of the grave were assumed to be remains of a C-Group superstructure. However, neither the rectangular slate palette nor the mirror with cordiform profile it contained is characteristic of the C-Group.[12] The mirror belongs to a category which Lilyquist has referred to as archaic,[13] and whatever its date, its tapered profile and bulged tang do not resemble those of mirrors that can be dated to the First Intermediate period and Middle Kingdom.[14] T 155 also contained a very small, almost biconical Egyptian jar with a flaring neck and slightly beaded rim. The vessel had apparently been made of alluvial clay and fired at a low or moderate temperature. Although it was almost black when found, the color is irregular, a feature which might have been produced in an open fire. The surface is still slightly lustrous. The closest parallels to this jar date to to the Old Kingdom.[15]

The second grave which also could not be dated to the A- or C-Groups was T 35. Although disturbed, this grave still contained two small, wide biconical jars with sharply carinated shoulders, flattened bases, short necks, and everted, beaded rims. These jars were also made of moderately fired alluvial clay. They have polished red coats that are, like the shape, characteristic of the Old Kingdom.[16] A copper axe, also from this grave, is a flat plate with a very slightly concave back. The edge, although curved, is not semicircular but subrectangular with rounded corners. Near the back of the blade is a small, square hole. Although axes having holes in this location have been approximately assigned various dates from the end of the Naqada period through the Archaic period,[17] this precise form of axe is known only from one dated context in Egypt, the tomb of Khasekhemwy at Abydos,[18] which was built several centuries after the end of the A-Group in Lower Nubia. Table 23 compares the major features of T 35 and T 155, and table 24 presents a number of tombs from other cemeteries that seem most likely to belong to the same period or group (see also table 25).

B. T 155, T 35, AND RELATED BURIALS IN LOWER NUBIA

The seven tombs identified in table 24 contained either evidence dating them to between the First and the Sixth Dynasties or evidence which grouped them with the burials in Cemetery T in table 23. Two were not identified with certainty because the publications do not give enough evidence to date them.

Of the three major groups that most resemble the two tombs in Cemetery T, 7.117 and 7.190 were originally assigned by Reisner to a period which he called the "Late B-Group." Neither of these tombs contained objects that are dated exclusively to the period between the Sixth and Twelfth Dynasties (C-Group I-IIA). However, the cordiform mirror, which does not resemble mirrors of these periods, indicates that tomb 7.117 dates to an earlier period. This type of mirror is the earliest of a series of metal mirrors, and it may have appeared as early as the late First Dynasty.[19] In any case, it is later than the A-Group proper, which ended as the First Dynasty was beginning. Tomb 7.190 contained an awl, adze, and axe. The adze differs from examples found in Djer's tomb at Saqqara;[20] its blade does not splay at the edge but curves inward. The axe, somewhat elongated, has a back with a very obtuse angle rather than a concavity. It would appear to be somewhat more

Table 23—Characteristics of T 35 and T 155

Superstructure:
    T 35:   row of gravel around the pit
    T 155:   line of larger stones around the pit

Stelae:
    T 155:   two stelae placed side by side outside the stones

Shaft:
    T 35:   broad oval, with large stones inside the shaft to protect the burial
    T 155:   rectangular with rounded corners to the north, rounded end to the south, hide or shield shaped

Burial:
    T 35:   N/—/—/—, disturbed
    T 155:   S/L/5/c, on hide

Objects:
    T 35:   2 red burnished carinated jars of Egyptian origin
              1 axe (compares with Dyn. II)
              1 blue fai. bead
    T 155:   1 small burnished jar (discolored) of Egyptian origin
              1 cordiform mirror
              1 round quartzite mortar with ochre, grindstone
              1 plano-convex, rectangular slate palette with bored, round hole, beveled edges, with black substance on the surface
              1 circular earring or hair-ring
              simple shell rings
              strings of beads strung on arms, neck, and both ankles

---

developed than the late Second Dynasty type found in T 35. Thus the copper tools and weapons from 7.190 differ from those of Djer, and the axe appears even more developed than those of Khasekhemwy and should perhaps be assigned a slightly later date. In addition, 209.1 should be considered approximately contemporary with T 155 because the two burials shared several unusual features.

C. COMMON FEATURES OF POST-A-GROUP BURIALS OF T 155/T 35 TYPE

Several objects dating to the Archaic period and later indicate that burials cited in tables 23 and 24 date to the time after the end of A-Group. It remains to be determined whether these burials represent an archaeological group of materials with characteristics which are distinct from those of the A- or C-Groups.

Table 24—Tombs to be Compared with T 35 and T 155

209.1[a]

    Shaft: oval

    Burial: S-E/L/knees semicontracted/hands before chest, head on fiber pillow

    Objects:

        1.   Globular pot of "brown ware"

        2.   Cordiform mirror wrapped in linen

        3.   Small "red ware" jar

        4.   Rectangular palette with beveled edges

        5.   Necklace of shell beads

        6.   Shell finger ring

        7.   Bracelet of shell, blue fai., and quartz beads

        8.   Three bone finger rings from right hand

     11.   Horn bracelet from left wrist

     12.   Bronze (copper) awl from below mirror

     13.   Anklet of mixed car. and shell beads, double strung

    Note that this group exhibits striking similarities to T 155 in the palette, mirror, awl, and use of bead strings on ankle, wrist, and neck.

7.117[b]

    Shaft: oval

    Burial: (N-) E/L/semicontracted/hands before face

    Objects:

        1.   Bag or mat

        2.   Cordiform mirror

        3.   Beads and amulet, including 100 gold (cylindrical) and 14 car.

        4.   Car. chip near neck

    Note that the mirror connects the group with T 155.

7.190[c]

    Shaft: oval; cut by Pan Grave

    Burial: (N-) E/L/semicontracted/hands before face

    Objects:

        1.   Copper awl

        2.   Copper adze with concave sides

        3.   Copper axe with semicircular blade

        4.   Six shell bracelets on right arm

        5.   V-shaped ivory armlet

        6.   Car. beads

        7.   Necklace of gold beads, 4 larger gold balls, and gold coil

    Note that nos. 2 and 3 relate the group to Early Dynastic; no. 3 dates to after Khasekhemwy. The gold coil from no. 7 could be Early Dynastic, and the V-shaped armlet is the type shown at Helwan.

41.206[d]

    Shaft: oval (N-S)

    Burial: cist

    Objects:

        1.   Carinated bowl of brown pottery

        2.   "Bright red-polished ware"

    Note that no. 2 may be Old Kingdom red polished pottery.

113/1.2[e]

    Shaft: oval

    Burial: E/R/contracted/hands before face

    Objects:

        1.   Rectangular slate palette

        2.   Mirror

        3.   Pottery palette

        4.   Pebble from no. 1

    Note that the combination of rectangular palette and mirror resembles T 155.

110.225[f]

    Shaft: denuded

    Burial: —

    Objects:

        1.   Large, blue glaze ball beads

        2.   Fragment of malachite or copper oxide

        3.   Copper mirror

      4-6.   Shell finger rings

        7.   Blue glaze, long oval bead

        8.   Small conus shells

        9.   Two amethyst ball beads

      10.   Small, shell disc beads

      11.   Car. fly amulets

      12.   Small ivory plaque with two holes for threading

      13.   Dumbbell-shaped ivory bead

      14.   Small, ball bead, blue glaze

      15.   Small beads, blue glaze

41.423[g]

    Object:

        1.   Cordiform mirror

    Note that this is a C-Group tomb. The mirror was probably reused.

---

[a]Emery and Kirwan 1935, p. 359.

[b]Reisner 1910, p. 46.

[c]Ibid., pp. 50-51.

[d]Ibid., p. 212.

[e]Firth 1927, p. 125.

[f]Ibid., p. 51.

[g]Reisner 1910, p. 223.

TOMB MARKED BY A ROW OF GRAVEL OR STONES (T 35, T 155, 47.423)

The row of stones or gravel around the pit is not characteristic of A-Group and not seen in early C-Group when superstructures were high, dry stone circles. Irregular surface marking of this kind occurs in the Pan Grave (P/1), Kerma, (K/1), and latest C-Group cultures.[21] Such a late date for these groups is precluded by the mirrors and axes cited in tables 23, 24, and 25.

SHAFT OVAL, HIDE-SHAPED, OR IRREGULAR (T 35, T 155, 4.206, 7.117, 7.190, 113.1, 209.1)

Simple oval shafts were made in all periods, especially for the burials of children. It is of interest to note, however, that all of the shafts in this group were hide-shaped,[22] oval, or irregular, and none were rectangular, or had parallel sides.

STONES IN THE SHAFT TO PROTECT BURIAL (T 35; [P/5])[23]

Apart from the stone blocking of great A-Group tombs, the use of stones in the shaft to protect the burial is not a typical feature of the A- or C-Groups. Later, it is a feature frequently found in burials of the Pan Grave culture.

BURIAL

The direction of the burial was either with the head to the south, with the body contracted on the left side (T 35 , T 155 , 209.1), or the head to the east, with the body contracted on either side (113.1, 7.117, 7.190). Neither of these orientations is especially distinctive.

GRAVE GOODS

The burials considered here were wealthy, containing considerable amounts of beads and metal goods. However, pottery, which was so important in both the A- and C-Group tombs, is not common, note, however, the Egyptian imports in T 155 and T 35 (small vessels). Beads were much more important than in the A-Group. Other objects, such as the cordiform mirror (T 155, 209.7, 7.117, 47.423, 113.1) and axe (T 35, 7.190) help set these tombs apart from A- and C-Group burials. One tomb (7.190) contained an armlet with a V-shaped profile which can be dated by representational evidence from Egypt; Fischer has pointed out the correspondence of this V-shaped armband and armbands shown worn by a man on a stela from the Archaic cemetery at Helwan. The armband, the man's distinctive hairstyle, and various aspects of his dress indicate the existence of a foreign group distinct from both the old A-Group and contemporary Egyptians.[24]

Many of the individual features identified above were not found exclusively in these burials, but considered as a group, these details appear to differentiate the burials from both A- and C-Group tombs. In any case, the graves found in Nubia in both the A- and C-Group periods have diverse aspects. In C-Group times, for example, the varied characteristics of burials allow distinct groups such as the C-Group, Pan Grave, and Kerma cultures to be identified. Moreover, the burials of A- and C-Group times also share important practices and even contain comparable objects. The existence of archaeological materials dating to the period between A- and C-Groups cannot be denied because the groups or burials that might be assigned to the intervening period are diverse or because they share some features with both the preceding and subsequent periods.

D. POST-A-GROUP OF T 155/T 35 TYPE AND GROUPS OF OTHER PERIODS

Insofar as any special cultural affinities with groups of later periods can be detected, then the tendency to make graves with curved, or even circular sides (P/1—as opposed to making graves with parallel sides) and the protective stones placed in the shaft (P/5) can be compared very generally to features of Pan Graves. In a still more tentative way, it might even be suggested that this group is related in some way to the simple slab-covered burials of the Qadan cemetery at Gebel Sahaba in the Cataract region.[25]

E. THE PERIOD AFTER A-GROUP IN LOWER NUBIA

One of the most difficult problems in the archaeology of Nubia is identifying remains from periods or cultures whose objects or burial customs are not distinctive.[26] For this very reason, evidence from important periods, such as the Twenty-Fifth Dynasty/Napatan periods,[27] the early Meroitic period,[28] and the later part of the New Kingdom,[29] has been disputed or ignored. It can be argued that the small number of groups identified above indicates that the phase was probably not one of substantial settlement. Although probably true, a statement of this kind could hardly be verified from the rudimentary publications now available, and the problem merits a retrospective examination of available records and materials. It might also be argued that these tombs represent a very specialized development in one of the major periods. However, the burials reviewed here were dispersed from one end of Lower Nubia to the other, giving this group a geographical as well as a temporal and cultural reality. Because Smith so carefully demonstrated the futility of assigning materials to a phase without evidence, it would not be reasonable on the basis of these tombs to re-establish a major B-Group with all or most of the tombs identified by Reisner and Firth. It is reasonable to believe, however, that the groups presented here represent a relatively wealthy core around which an uncertain number of other groups may be clustered.[30]

Although the evidence does not indicate a dense population, it is clear that there was a population in Lower Nubia between the A- and C- Groups. The burial customs, the kinds of grave goods they used, and the hairstyles indicate that these people represented a distinct cultural group.[31]

F. REGISTER OF FINDS

Table 25—Register of Post-A-Group Burials at Adindan

		FIGURE	PLATE
T 35		70	55
Superstructure: gravel distributed in semicircle S, E-SE of shaft			
Shaft: oval, 1.20 × .75 × .75 m		70a	
Burial: —			
Body: adult female			
Objects:			
1. Red-polished Egyptian jar 2.5 YR 5/6	23327	70d	53b
2. Same	23326	70e	53a
3. Blue fai. bead[a]	samp.	70b	
4. Copper axe	23299	70c	53c
T 155		71	51
Superstructure: row of stones along the NE side of the shaft			
Stelae: remains of 2, sandstone against stone row to north			
Shaft: rect. with rounded N end, rounded S corners; shield-shaped		71a	
Burial: S/L/5/c, on hide, remains at pelvis and feet			
Body: adult female			
Objects:			
1. Small, burnished Egyptian jar, black discoloration	23337	71i	54a
2. Fragments of malachite	same		54c
3. Large, stone palette with ochre residue, quartzite	23371		54f
4. Pestle (near hand)	same		54f
5. a. Cordiform mirror	23379	71b	53d
b. Fur below mirror	disc.		
c. Matting below fur	disc.		
6. Copper awl or kohl stick	23386	71j	54d
7. 2 pebbles (for grinding?, near right hand)	samp.	71g-h	54b
8. Rect. plano-convex, slate palette with beveled edges and pebble for grinding; black stain on upper surface	23387A-B	71c, e	54e
9. Ring (on right index finger), shell	23385	71d	52f
10. Ost. egg. bead bracelet in three loops (right arm)[a]	23380	71k	52a
a. ost. egg. size 1 276			
b. blue fai., dk. size 1 1			
c. blue fai dk., short cyl. 3			

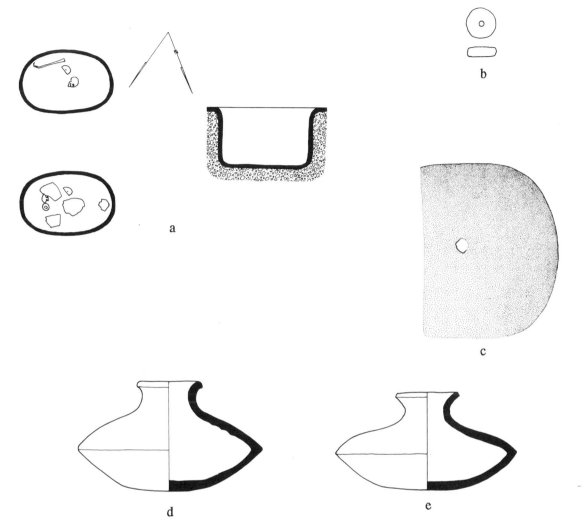

Figure 70. T 35: (a) Plan and section; (b) Bead, no. 3; (c) Copper axe, no. 4; Pottery— (d) No. 1; (e) No. 2. Scale 2:5 except (a) 1:50, (b) 2:1.

Table 25—Register of Post-A-Group Burials at Adindan — Cont.

				FIGURE	PLATE
T 155 — Cont.					
11. Necklace of beads[a]			23381	71m	52c
	a.	ost. egg. size 1-3	91		
	b.	blue-gn. fai dk. size 1	19		
	c.	same, size 3	37		
	d.	same, short cyl.	23		
	e.	same, long cyl.	3		

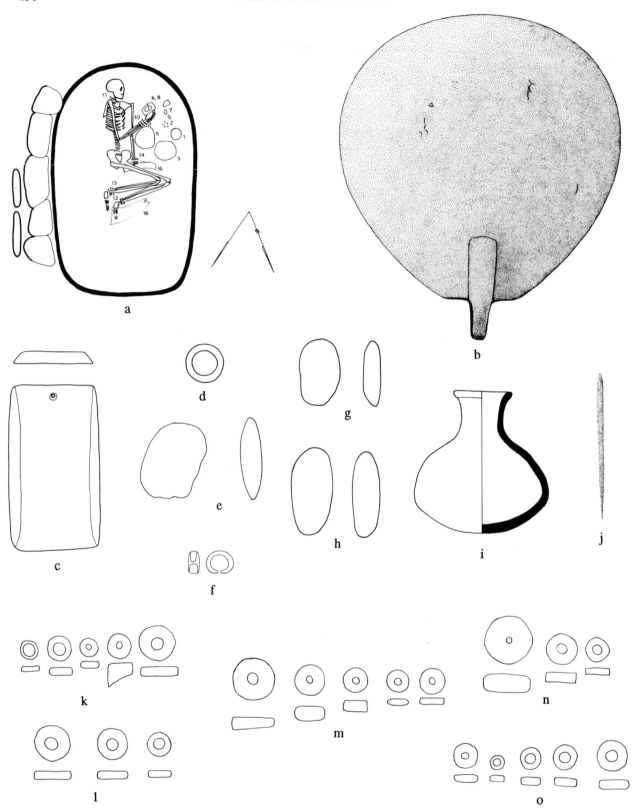

Figure 71. T 155: (a) Plan; (b) Mirror, no. 5; (c) Palette, no. 8a; (d) Ring, no. 9; (e) Pebble, no. 8b; (f) Earring or hair-ring, no. 15; Pebbles— (g) No. 7a; (h) No. 7b; (i) Pottery jar, no. 1; (j) Copper pin, no. 6; Beads— (k) Bracelet, no. 10; (l) Anklet, no. 13; (m) Necklace, no. 11; (n) Bracelet, no. 14; (o) Anklet, no. 12. Scale (a) 1:50, (b-j) 2:5, (k-o) 2:1.

Table 25—Register of Post-A-Group Burials at Adindan — Cont.

			FIGURE	PLATE
T 155 — Cont.				
12. Anklet of beads (on left leg)[a]		23382	71o	52b
a. ost. egg. size 2-3	194			
b. bl. fai. size 1-2	4			
13. Anklet of beads (on right leg) in three loops[a]		23384	71l	52e
a. ost. egg.	235			
14. Bracelet of beads (from left arm) in three loops[a]		23383	71n	52d
a. ost. egg.	180			
b. blue fai.	3			
15. Shell earring or hair-ring		samp.	71f	52g
16. Leather remains under body		disc.		
17. Stelae fragments (2) beside stone superstructure		disc.		

Note that other tombs such as T 11, T 243, and T 247, which are presented in the A-Group register, have features not entirely consistent with the early date of A-Group, but the evidence is insufficient to assign them with confidence to a later period.

---

[a] For the typology of beads, see *OINE* III, pp. 120-21; and *OINE* V, table 40, p. 83.

NOTES

1. Smith 1966.

2. Ibid., pp. 74-86.

3. Ibid., p. 95. This includes a discussion of Cemetery 50: 100-110.

4. Ibid., pp. 95-97. Other changes in Firth's criteria are noted on pp. 98-109.

5. Ibid., pp. 118-19.

6. Ibid., p. 119, ". . . few if any burials were made during these five hundred years or more . . ."

7. Ibid., p. 121 for the end of A-Group; for the gap, see pp. 118-19. See Petrie 1920, p. 17, for early remarks on the Reisner chronology.

8. For a recent discussion of the political geography of Nubia in the Sixth Dynasty, see O'Connor 1986.

9. For a discussion of this issue, see Mayer-Thurman and Williams 1979, pp. 20 and 25. See also Williams 1985, pp. 149-50.

10. Smith 1966, p. 71.

11. For a general discussion, see *OINE* V, chapter 1, pp. 1-22.

12. The characteristic cosmetic of the C-Group was galena; it was normally placed in a caked, ground form in shells of the Nile clam *Etheria elliptica* (*OINE* V, pp. 75-76). The grindstones are circular or oval (ibid. 76; see also Steindorff 1935, pl. 68, below; see the mirrors in pl. 69). Of the number of mirrors found in Lower Nubia of this type (Lilyquist 1971; see also 1979—without much of the information on Nubia) appearing in table 20, only that in 41.423 was found in a C-Group tomb. Other mirrors found in C-Group burials were of the usual Middle Kingdom shapes. Lilyquist believes that the cordiform mirror Aswan 734 actually came from 110.225, which contained a mirror of unspecified shape (110.225-iii); the piece in Aswan was labeled 7/223/iii.

13. Lilyquist 1979, pp. 4-5.

14. Ibid., passim.

15. Reisner 1955; necks with beaded rims are common (fig. 93), as are globular to biconical bodies (figs. 86, 87, and 93).

16. The closest parallel for either these carinated jars or the more globular example from T 155 is from Giza (ibid., fig. 91: 33-2-122). A small carinated jar with a short neck and rolled rim was found in a badly disturbed area of Cemetery K. (*OINE* V, p. 220, K 70D—1, pls. 74F and 84F). The jar was worn and badly discolored above the carination, making an accurate color reading impossible, but evidence of burnishing could still be seen. The vessel was assigned to the hard pink category in *OINE* V, but at least some alluvial clay was present because some of the mica typically found in these clays is visible on the surface. Although the jar can be dated to before C-Group, the findspot does not; earlier imported pottery was redeposited as grave goods in this period (*OINE* V, p. 209, K 33—2).

17. For a typology of early axes, see W. Davies 1987, especially pp. 27-29 for axes from the Naqada period and the First Dynasty. See also Baumgartel 1960, pp. 13-14.

18. W. Davies 1987, pp. 28-29, has a detailed discussion of axes of this kind from the tomb of Khasekhemwy at Abydos, including both full-sized examples and models (cats. 6-11). The evidence for dating axes with a single hole for hafting is discussed in detail on pp. 29-30. Models of axes with single holes continued to be made into the Sixth Dynasty, but their shapes differ from the Second Dynasty axes. See also Petrie 1901, pl. XLV: 76.

19. Lilyquist 1971, p. 45; idem 1979, pp. 4-5.

20. Reisner 1910, p. 50, pl. 65: b8 and 9. Forms of adzes are reviewed by Baumgartel (1960, pp. 12 and 13) and Petrie (1917, pl. XV, pp. 16-17). Naqada period adzes are rectangular or slightly trapezoidal plates, sometimes rounded at one end and, by the time of the First Dynasty, occasionally splayed at the edge with a more or less concave side (Emery 1949, pp. 37-38, pl. 10, from Tomb 3471 of Djer's time). Some have squared and others rounded heads. See also Emery 1954, pl. XXXI b, from tomb 3504 of Djer's time. The profile of later adzes is sinuous; the side curves inward below the rounded head, then outward and inward again just above the cutting edge. This shape, that of the adze from 7.190, seems to date to the early Old Kingdom or to the end of the Second through the Third Dynasties (Petrie 1917, p. 16, pls. XV-XVI; Garstang 1903). The Fourth Dynasty type has a stop at the base of the head (Petrie 1917, pl. XVII, 76; Reisner 1942, pl. 58f, and fig. 279, 13-11-16).

21. Bietak 1968, pp. 113, 118, and 123.

22. Placing burials on a hide, often in hide-shaped or shield-shaped shafts, as in the case of T 155, was an important mode of interment at Kerma before the latest phase. Burials of this type were replaced by the bed burial. See Bonnet 1982, figs. 16-19; Dunham 1982, figs. 146, 152, 155-57, 160, 164, 167, 199, 203, 206, 213, 214, 228, 232, 234, and 239. Only a few of the burials excavated by Reisner were in hide-shaped shafts; most graves were round.

23. Bietak 1968, p. 119. For a rare occurrence of this feature in A-Group, see Smith 1962, fig. 14 (Tunqala West).

24. Fischer 1963, pp. 35-39.

25. See Wendorff and Schild et al. 1984, especially the conclusion. This suggestion is tentative not only because of the substantial chronological gap between Qadan and the later Archaic period, but also because of the simple nature of the feature. There is also a substantial chronological gap between the two periods. However, Abkan was very possibly derived from Qadan (Nordström 1972, p. 17), and Abkan traditions in pottery manufacturing, for example, continued, only partially assimilated, in A-Group. There is therefore some reason to believe that the cultures of these successive periods were related even though they may not have succeeded one another directly. See also Wendorff 1968.

26. For example, a cemetery of two small tomb clusters found by the Soviet expedition at Koshtamna near Khor-Daud contained materials that were compared to the so-called B-Group, especially Cemetery 7, knoll B at Shellal (Vinogradov 1964, pp. 206-18). This cemetery could not be assigned to any of the archaeological phases or groups now recognized: A-Group, C-Group, Pan-Grave, Kerma, Egyptian, or any later phase. The pottery was unremarkable; most pieces would not stand out in any C- or, to a lesser extent, A-Group context. However, these pottery vessels, as a group, can be distinguished from both phases quite easily. Most of the vessels, all of them beakers or bowls, can be found in Petrie's (1920, pl. 1) corpus of black-topped vessels, but most of Petrie's examples came from Nubia (see Vinogradov 1964, figs. 4: 1-3; 5: 1-4, 7-11). The two black-topped beakers (ibid., fig. 5: 5-6) appear quite early (Petrie 1921, pl. 2: 18-19).
   Although the oval gravel-ring superstructures and deep oval or circular shafts (one containing a dog) do not contrast with the present group of burials, they indicate only very general cultural associations. The same could be said about the very simple objects from grave 1 (Vinogradov 1964, fig. 4): stone implements, a needle, simple beads, and a cowrie. The only strong chronological evidence are the beakers, which indicate an early date. The Koshtamna cemeteries can be regarded as poor contemporaries of the early A-Group, without the imports or elaborate objects often found in that culture (see Reisner 1910, pp. 314-22).

27. Vila 1979, p. 37; idem 1980, especially pp. 175-78; *OINE* VII (forthcoming).

28. Williams 1985.

29. Holthoer 1977, see pls. 25: CU 1 and 26: CU 5, which Holthoer dates to the late New Kingdom.

30. Despite the lack of large pottery vessels, these tombs were quite rich. Copper implements of the size found in most of these graves would not be found in more than one in one hundred A-Group or one in several hundred C-Group tombs. I have not assigned poor graves to the group because, as emphasized by Smith, the poorer graves are not readily distinguished from A-Group, C-Group, or Pan Grave burials. But the existence of these rather wealthy graves implies the existence of a contemporary, poorer population in the same area, however sparse.

31. For the hairstyle, see Fischer 1963, pp. 35-39, figs. 1-3.

4

CONCLUSION

Although the record of occupation is as discontinuous in this part of Nubia as elsewhere, exploration has been extensive, and it permits a few conclusions. For the period covered by this and the previous volume (*OINE* III) in all areas of Lower Nubia, from the late Neolithic to the Old Kingdom, the most striking feature is that more sites can be attributed to A-Group than any other period.

A. SETTLEMENT IN NUBIA BEFORE C-GROUP TIMES

In the time of the Abkan and related Sudanese Neolithic cultures, the Second Cataract region and the area just to the south was settled only sparsely, and there is very little evidence of occupation further north between the cataract and the early A-Group settlements just south of Aswan. Even in the area where Abkan materials have been found, the evidence is sparse. The Scandinavian Joint Expedition found only five sites in its large concession.[1] Seven were located by the combined Prehistoric Expedition,[2] and six or seven more were found on the west bank.[3] These sites can be added to the few known before[4] and the cave behind Cemetery K to comprise the record of the Abkan culture north of Dal. Despite innovations in herding, agriculture, and fishing,[5] the occupation of Lower Nubia near the cataract was hardly denser in the late Neolithic than it had been earlier. Evidence for Neolithic settlement is absent farther north in Lower Nubia.[6]

The great change came with the appearance of the A-Group culture, which significantly increased the density of occupation in Lower Nubia and established hierarchical pharaonic institutions. At the same time, A-Group encompassed elements of several traditions, a mixture apparent in the materials presented here and in the previous volume. The combination of cultures and proliferating settlements began late in the Middle A-Group and continued through the Late A-Group, probably not lasting more than four centuries.[7] By the early First Dynasty, the A-Group culture seems to have ended abruptly, and evidence of occupation after that time is minimal, as indicated in the previous chapter. The chronological evidence gleaned from the tombs of this Post-A-Group phase (of T 155/T 35 type) indicates that it dates to the later Archaic period and possibly the early Old Kingdom — giving some archaeological background for Sneferu's record of booty from Nubia. The most important sites with evidence of occupation or activity in the region from the Fourth through the Sixth Dynasties were the Buhen settlement and the quarries.[8]

Despite a generally increasing number of sites in Nubia and adjacent regions, evidence for settlement in Lower Nubia was, down to the end of the Fifth Dynasty, rather sparse. The important A-Group presence was exceptional. Before the appearance of A-Group, Nubia had been part of a shifting regional pattern of occupation which included two major regions. The first consisted of sites at scattered "playas" in the desert and areas at the bases of major outcrops fairly far to the west. The second was made up of sites in and near the valley.[9]

135

Rather than ecological changes, which seem to have been less substantial in this period than at other times,[10] it appears that the A-Group's rapid rise represented the exploitation of new opportunities offered by the great expansion of the Naqada culture in Egypt. It is interesting that a similar rapid increase in activity occurred at the same time in the trading settlements of Sinai. The end of this major episode in Nubia also coincided with the end of the Sinai settlements, a coincidence that may be attributed to political consolidation in Egypt, explicitly expressed in the claim of Hor-Aha "smiting Ta-Seti."[11] Thereafter, Lower Nubia once again became sparsely populated.[12]

The large-scale survey of remains from Dal to Sai has revealed little evidence of the so-called Khartoum Variant and Abkan; some sites were identified as Early Nubian, but the materials are not the same as those of the A-Group in Lower Nubia. However, far to the south, the Shendi Reach contains major sites that date to this and the preceding period. The most important are the Neolithic cemeteries of Kadada and el-Ghaba at Taragma less than 40 km south of Meroe. While the complete body of chronological evidence is not yet available, it is clear that some sites were as large and concentrated as many found in the Naqada culture of Upper Egypt. The Neolithic culture of Sudan — which extended northward into the Dongola Reach — may have played a much more important role in both A-Group and the Naqada culture than previously supposed.[13] After A-Group, the next period of intensive settlement in Lower Nubia occurred in the Sixth Dynasty when the C-Group appeared.[14] Coincidentally, this also occurred as changes in Egypt offered new opportunities to the population.

B. SUDANESE NEOLITHIC, ABKAN, A-GROUP,
AND THE NEOLITHIC OF UPPER EGYPT

Although the cave behind Cemetery K is the northernmost site that can be included in the Abkan culture, it is not that culture's northernmost connection. Kaiser has identified a widespread, if sparsely distributed, Neolithic culture in Upper Egypt,[15] which he identified as a Tasian culture extending far beyond the confines of Middle Egypt where it was first identified. This greater Tasian culture had important relations with the Neolithic cultures of Sudan and the Sahara. These relations are emphasized in a striking way by the appearance of flared incised beakers in the Sudanese Neolithic burials at Kadada near Shendi[16] and a small model beaker in a burial at Nabta in the Western Desert near Lower Nubia.[17] The description of Tasian pottery matches that of Abkan more than any other archaeological group in Lower Nubia or Upper Egypt, although we know little of pottery shapes before A-Group in Lower Nubia.[18] However, the shapes of A-Group pottery often closely resemble those of Tasian, and the entire corpus presented by Kaiser could be added to A-Group without any of the vessels (except for the flared beakers) appearing unusual (see table 25 below). This does not indicate a synchronism, for these vessels all have shapes too simple to indicate more than just a general relationship. Although Kaiser also attempted to relate Middle Egypt's other Neolithic culture, the Badarian, to materials in Nubia, his greater Tasian culture is at least as closely related to the cultures of Nubia as the Badarian.

The archaeological evidence from Upper Egypt is neither dense nor definitive, but it is reasonable to reconstruct a very sparse settlement for the region during the Late Neolithic along lines suggested by Kaiser.[19] The interrelations among the various Upper Egyptian archaeological groups are not a subject for discussion here, but it is reasonable to note that during this period the density of occupation reconstructed for Upper Egypt is hardly more than the Second Cataract area. The relationship between the culture of Upper Egyptian

Neolithic and those of contemporary Nubia and Sudan was strong enough for these cultures to be included in the same cultural sphere. The significant features these cultures shared continued to be recognizable in Nubia for some time.

Table 26 —Shapes of Tasian Pottery and A-Group Counterparts

Kaiser 1985 (corpus)	*OINE* IV (figure)	Nordström 1972 (figure) and other Sudan sites
6: 38, 39	6: c (rippled) 7: g (fine)	41: AIV-3 brown/red rippled 43: AIX-26 black top red-pol.
6: 46, 47	9: j (here pointed)	41: AVIIe brown/black pol.
6: 54h	9: h (ord.)	37: AIe-8 brown coarse or smooth
6: 17, 49	9: d (ord.) 7: b (fine)	36: AI, 25-26
6: 4M		(various oval vessels in Nubia)
7: 20, 26	2: b-c (Abkan)	39: AIII (various)
7: 26	6: e (rippled, wider) 7: j (fine)	
7: 33	6: m (rippled)	
7: 1 (rect.)	7: 1 (triangular)	37: AIb, 8
7: 42 (carinated)		40: AIIIe, 2
7: 62 (zigzags on rim)	2: d (shape differs)	Other Sudan sites[a]
7: 63; 8: 1-3		Other Sudan and Desert sites[b]

[a]The specific combination of designs does not occur in early Nubia, but the general kind of design is typical. For incised vessels of this shape, see Geus 1976, pl. IX, nos. 3-4, and for combinations of different designs, see pl. X. Combinations of this kind are very common on A-Group painted pottery; see *OINE* III, table 9, pp. 31-60.

[b]Geus and Reinold 1979, fig. 22; Geus 1981, fig. 5a; idem 1976, pl. X; idem 1980, fig. 4, pl. VII; and idem 1983, pl. VII c, all from the Shendi area. See also Reinold 1987, pp. 29-34, especially fig. 4: E.R, and p. 51, fig. 11, from Kadruka in the Dongola Reach. For a small model of a flared beaker from Nabta Playa in the Western Desert near Lower Nubia, see Wendorff and Schild et al. 1980, fig. 3.109.

C. CEMETERY S, CEMETERY L, AND THE SEQUENCE OF ROYAL COMPLEXES

The early relationships of Neolithic and A-Group cultures with Egypt are not the only aspects of special interest in these early remains. *OINE* III presented Cemetery L as a royal cemetery.[20] In that volume, it was noted that pharaonic royal tombs consisted not only of the great tomb itself, but of complexes with various elements. Kaiser and Dreyer, in their re-examination of the Abydos royal cemetery of Dynasties 0, I, and II, traced a sequential development of two major parts of the complex: the royal tombs in a group in the desert and lower complexes at the edge of the valley which were also located in a group; they occurred slightly to the north of a direct east-west axis leading from the river to the royal tomb. Apart from subsidiary burials associated with both the tomb and the lower complexes, it was clear that the central feature of the lower, or valley, complex was a paneled structure. The latest examples were constructed of brick, but the earlier ones, located in rectangles of subsidiary burials, must have been made of more perishable materials. Using the design of the brick structures (and Djoser's enclosure at Saqqara) as a guide, the facades of the valley complexes could be reconstructed as *serekh* or palace facades;[21] they were faced with matting and posts or some representational equivalent of the palace facade. In *OINE* III, the development of the royal complex as a whole was traced in reverse chronological order to a pair of tombs (one surrounded with postholes) forming a single complex at Hierakonpolis, which dated to the beginning of Dynasty 0 and finally to Cemetery L at Qustul in the preceding Naqada IIIa. Only the royal tomb and accompanying cattle sacrifices were found, but there were representations of the palace facade on incense burners that may well have depicted *heb sed* courts or valley enclosures.[22]

The unusual deposit pits or shafts in Cemetery S are contemporary with Cemetery L and date to the late A-Group. The rectangular shafts have the same orientation as the great tombs in Cemetery L, and they are located to the north of an east-west axis leading from the river to the cemetery (fig. 72). No sign of superstructures was detected, and none was sought; one shaft, however, did contain a piece of stone which may have been a stela. The significance of the shafts and their relation to Cemetery L is problematic, but there is a possible explanation. Stadelmann has proposed that great Second Dynasty substructure complexes south of the Djoser complex at Saqqara be identified not as royal tombs themselves, but as "Buto Tombs," tombs associated with large royal enclosures located to the west. He also indicated that the long magazine complexes located nearby, at the west side of the Djoser complex, may belong not to Djoser, but to the last ruler of the Second Dynasty, Khasekhemwy.[23] If such large substructure complexes had existed in the Second Dynasty between the main paneled enclosure and the river, it would be reasonable to suppose that they had an earlier period of development (as did the large paneled structures traced by Kaiser and Dreyer). In this case, the Cemetery S shafts could then be identified as simple antecedents of the great complexes excavated at Saqqara in the Second Dynasty.

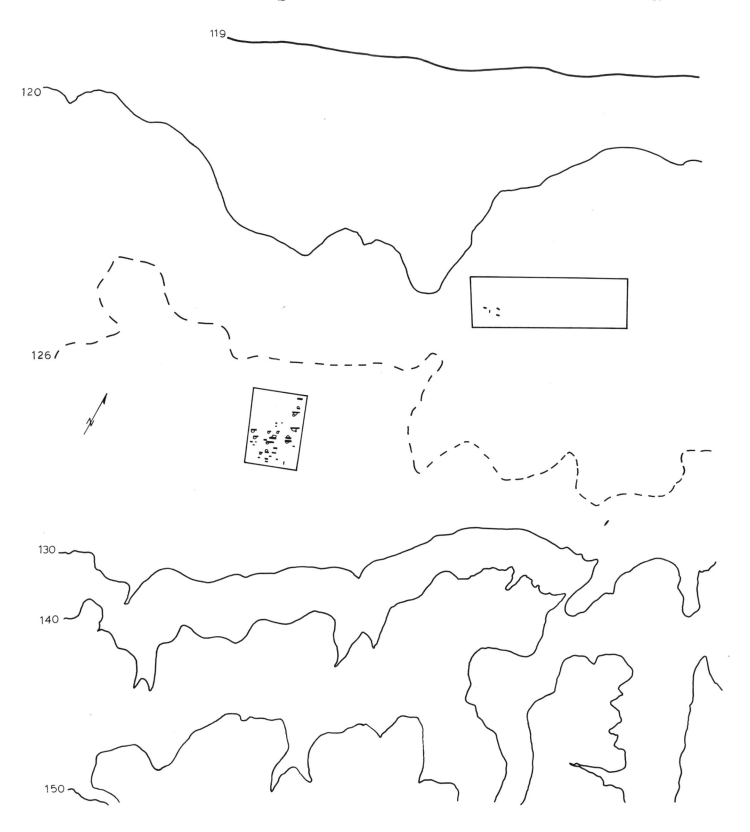

Figure 72. Sketch-plan of Cemeteries L and S. No scale.

NOTES

1. Nordström 1972, p. 13.

2. Ibid., pp. 12–13.

3. Ibid., p. 13.

4. Myers 1958, 1960.

5. This is the so-called Nilotic adjustment.

6. The concentration of the Neolithic in the cataract region compares with A-Group's settlement of every major usable area along the river in Lower Nubia explored to date. The increase in the number of sites may have been moderate in the cataract region, but the increase in sites in Lower Nubia is generally very substantial. Egyptian pottery from Middle and Late A-Group in this region dates to Naqada III (*OINE* III, pp. 9–13).

7. For a correlation with the Naqada Period, see *OINE* III, p. 13, table 3.

8. Emery 1963. See also Smith 1966, p. 120.

9. Wendorff and Schild et al. 1984; see pp. 404–28 for a general discussion of the Neolithic in the area and pp. 427–28 for the Late Neolithic.

10. Ibid., pp. 404–28.

11. Petrie 1901, pls. III, 2; XI, 1. See also Helck 1987, p. 145. For the Sinai route, see Oren 1973. The date of the trans-Sinai trade is probably earlier than that indicated by Oren. See *OINE* III, p. 175, for the date of the Ein Besor sealings, for example.

12. Continued campaigning is indicated by the well-known reference to booty of Nubia in the records of Sneferu on the Palermo Stone. This entry in the annals is possibly more significant than single references might otherwise be, since the records are so fragmentary. However, the strong evidence for trade in the tombs of Lower Nubia in the Archaic period coupled with the representation of a person from Nubia in native dress with his own jewelry and hairstyle indicate that relations were probably largely peaceful during this period.

13. Vila 1979, pp. 25–27. The "Early Nubian" sites south of Malik al-Nasir are not A-Group but belong to the Sudanese tradition. For sites in the Shendi Reach, see Reinold 1987, especially pp. 18–34 and fig. 1 (Kadada cemetery and chronology); ibid, pp. 41–43 and Lecointre 1987, especially figs. 2–3 (el-Ghaba cemetery). For Kadruka in the Dongola Reach, see Reinold 1987, pp. 50–53.

14. See O'Connor 1986 for a review of the evidence for political geography in Nubia during this period. Yam has been proposed as an antecedent of Kush (Trigger 1965, p. 95), but the name may have been applied to an area further south (O'Connor 1986, pp. 39–42).

15. Kaiser 1985a, pp. 71–85.

16. Geus 1976, pl. X.

17. Wendorff and Schild et al. 1980, p. 164, fig. 3.109.

18. See p. 4, fig. 2:a–d above, see also Nordström 1972, pp. 47–50, 57–60 and 80 for Abkan pottery generally. Cf. the remarks of Kaiser 1985a, pp. 73–76. The irregularly fired surfaces are noteworthy.

19. See Kaiser 1985a, pp. 71–79. All the sites assigned to the period are small or very poorly preserved.

20. *OINE* III, pp. 163–85.

21. *OINE* III, pp. 175–77 and table 42; Kaiser and Dreyer 1982, pp. 255–58. See also Kaiser 1985b.

22. *OINE* III, p. 176, pl. 34.

23. For the reconstructed arrangement of Second Dynasty complexes at Saqqara, see Stadelmann 1985, especially p. 306, fig. 3.

PLATE 1

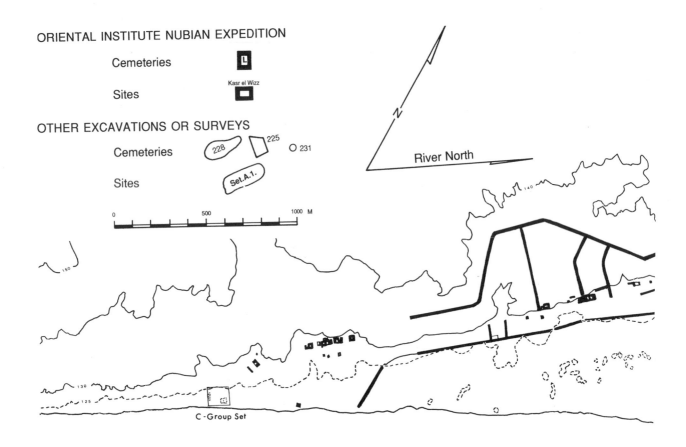

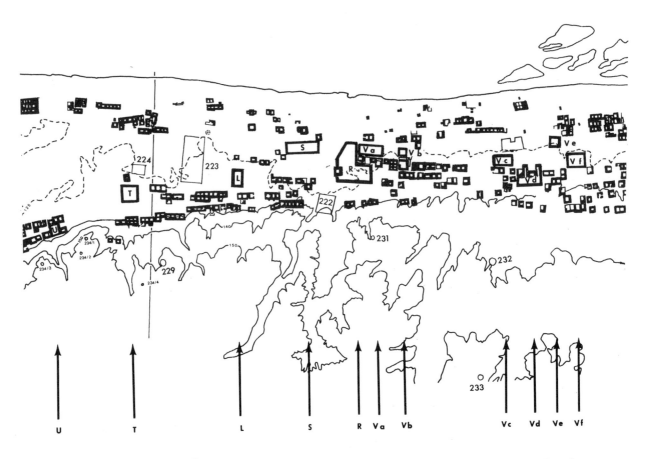

Operations of the Oriental Institute Nubian Expedition between Abu Simbel and the Sudan Frontier.

PLATE 2

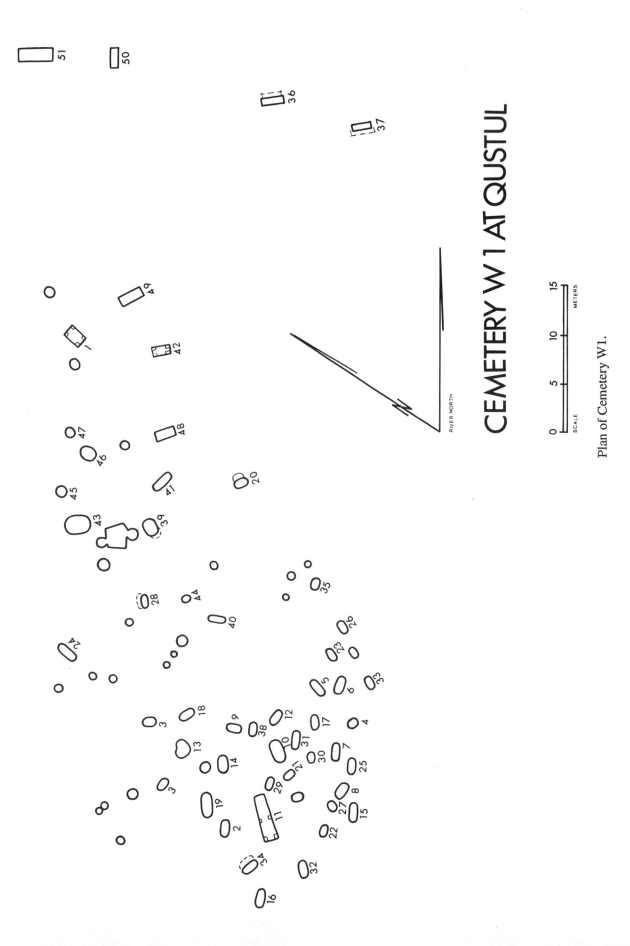

CEMETERY W 1 AT QUSTUL

Plan of Cemetery W1.

PLATE 3

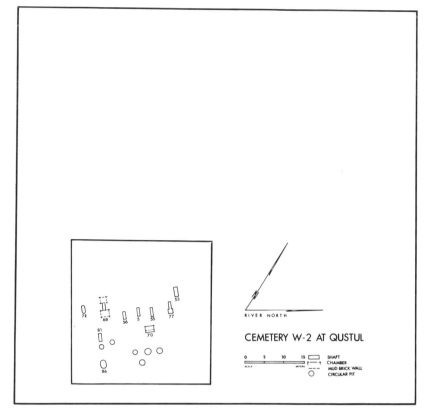

CEMETERY W-2 AT QUSTUL

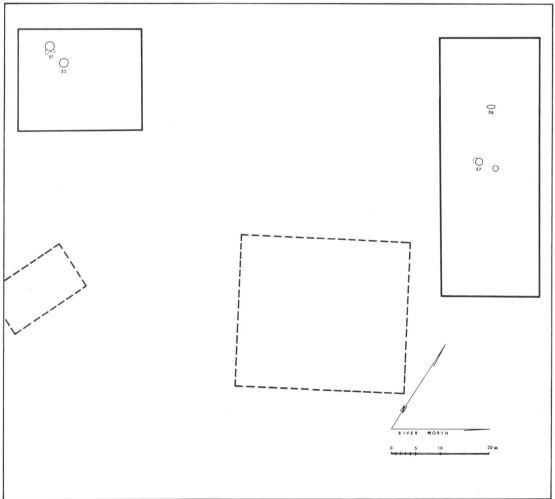

Plans: Cemeteries W2 and Vd, A-Group areas with key plans.

PLATE 4

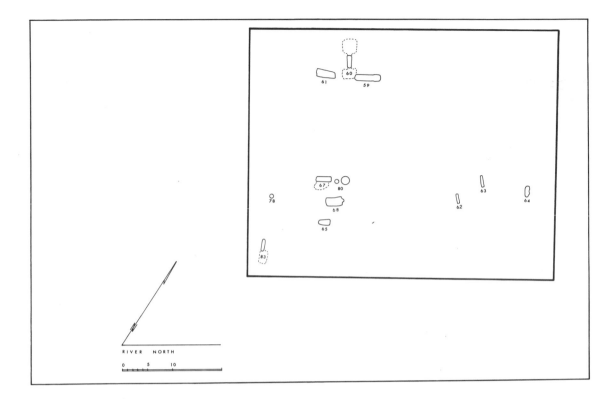

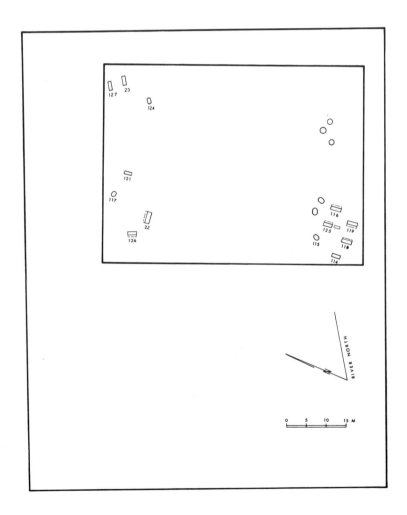

Plans: Cemeteries Vf and Vh, A-Group areas with key plans.

PLATE 5

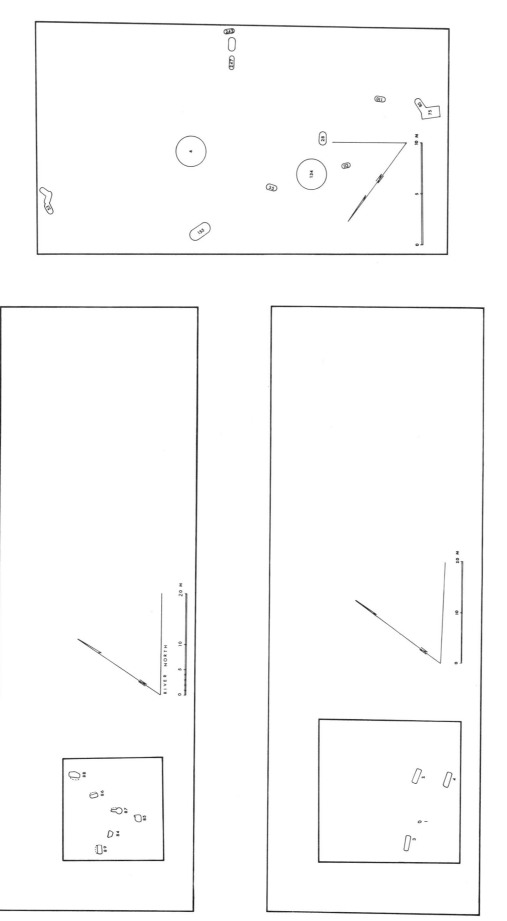

Plans: Cemeteries Vg and S, A-Group areas and key plans; Cemetery T, A-Group, and post-A-Group tombs.

PLATE 6

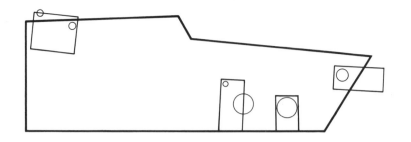

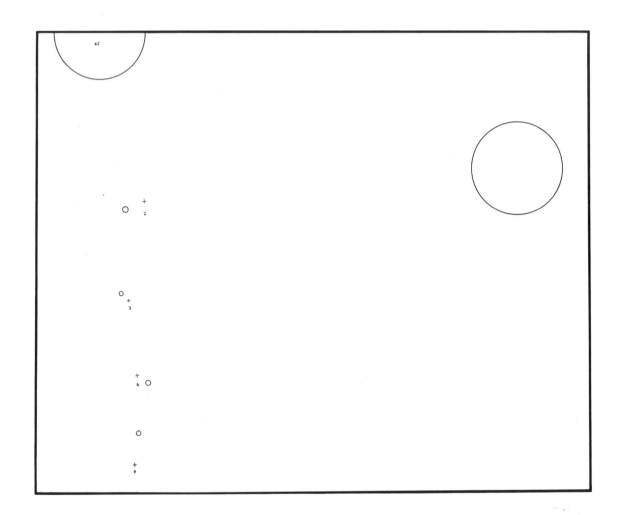

Plans of Cemetery Q, southwest A-Group area and key plan.

+ indicates the location of
a numbered late shaft

PLATE 7

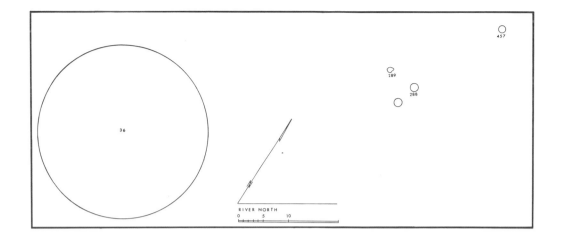

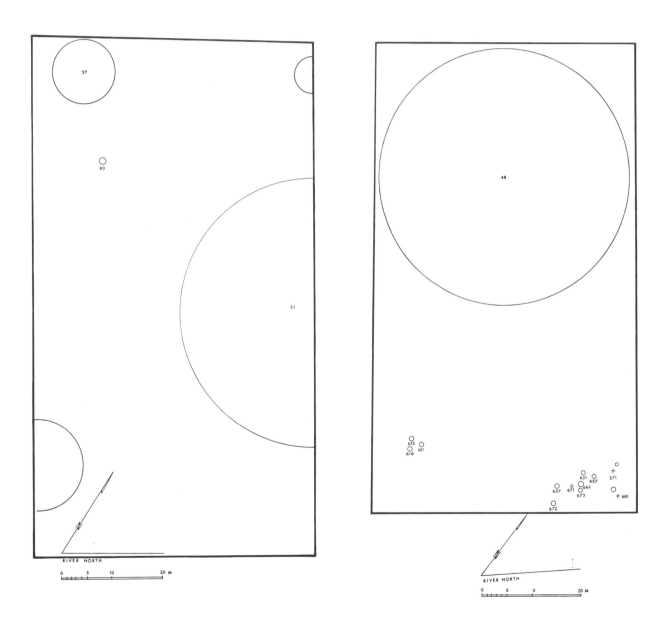

Plans of Cemetery Q, north, south-central, and central A-Group areas.

PLATE 8

An ostrich eggshell from the cave east of Cemetery K: no. 17. Scale ca. 1:1.

PLATE 9

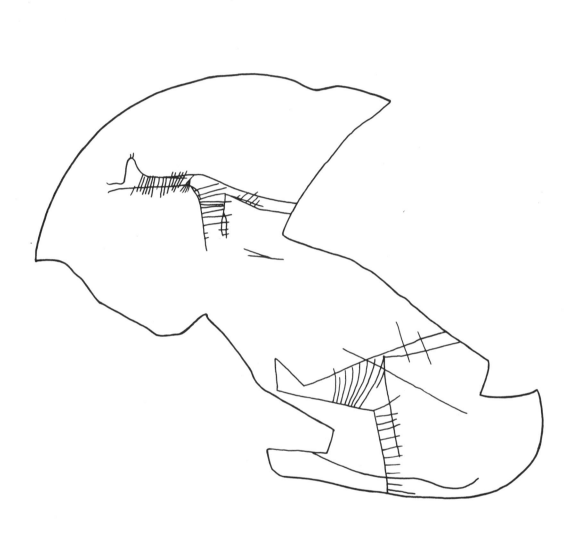

An ostrich eggshell from the cave east of Cemetery K: no. 17. Scale 1:1. The shape is distorted to show the second giraffe.

PLATE 10

Fragments of ostrich eggshell from the cave: (a) No. 17; (b) No. 21; No. 19; No. 18; (c) No. 22. Scale 1:1.

PLATE 11

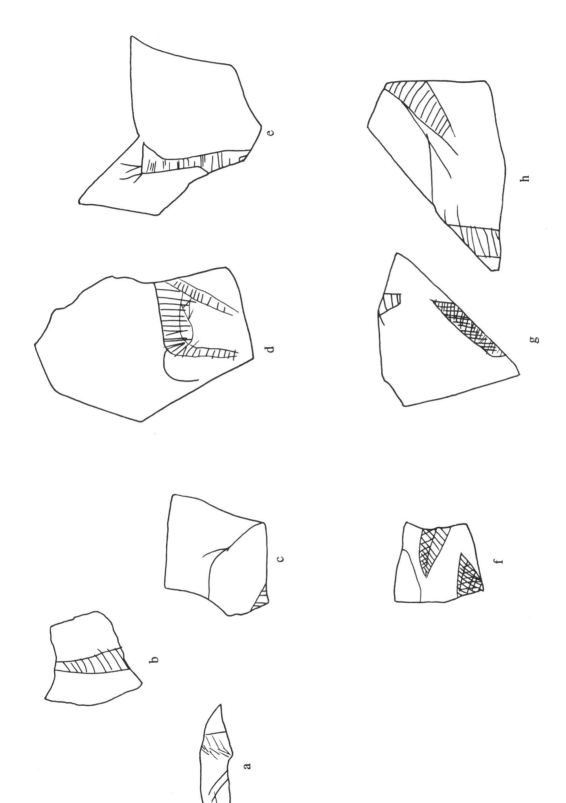

Fragments of ostrich eggshell from the cave: (a) No. 20; (b) No. 21; (c) No. 23; (d) No. 19; (e) No. 18; (f-h) No. 22. Scale 1:1.

PLATE 12

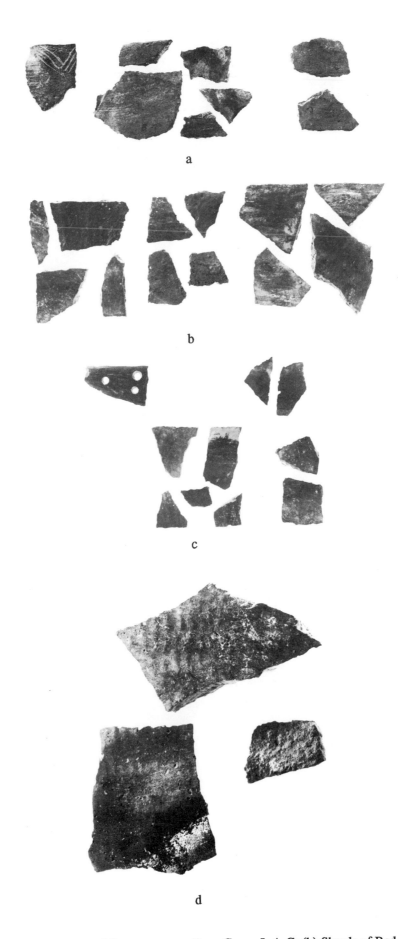

a

b

c

d

Pottery from the cave: (a) Sherds of Coarse pottery, Form Group I, A-C; (b) Sherds of Red-Coated pottery, Form Group II, A-C; (c) Sherd of Black Polished pottery, Form Group III, A and Sherds of Dark Brown and Black Polished pottery, Form Group IV A-C; (d) Sherds of Rippled pottery, Form Group V, A. Scale ca. 2:5.

PLATE 13

a

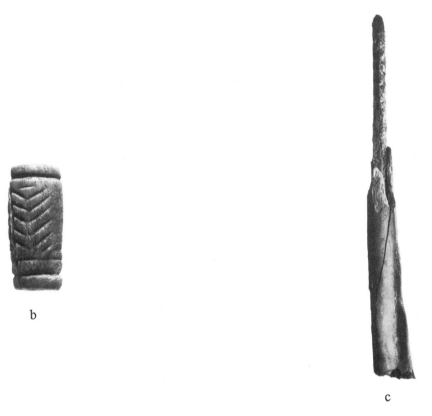

b

c

Objects from the cave and from A-Group tombs: (a) Objects from the cave, nos. 2, 1, 3, 5; (b) Ivory cylinder seal, W 2—6; (c) Copper awl mounted in bone, W 38—4. Scale (a) ca. 1:2, (b), (c) 1:1.

PLATE 14

A-Group Exterior Painted pottery, Form Group I: (a) W 10—12; (b) W 19—4; (c) W 19—12; (d) W 10—2; (e) W 11—6. Scale ca. 2:5.

PLATE 15

A-Group Exterior Painted pottery, Form Group I: (a) W 10—3; (b) W 11—10; (c) W 19—15; (d) W 10—4; (e) W 11—4. Scale ca. 2:5.

PLATE 16

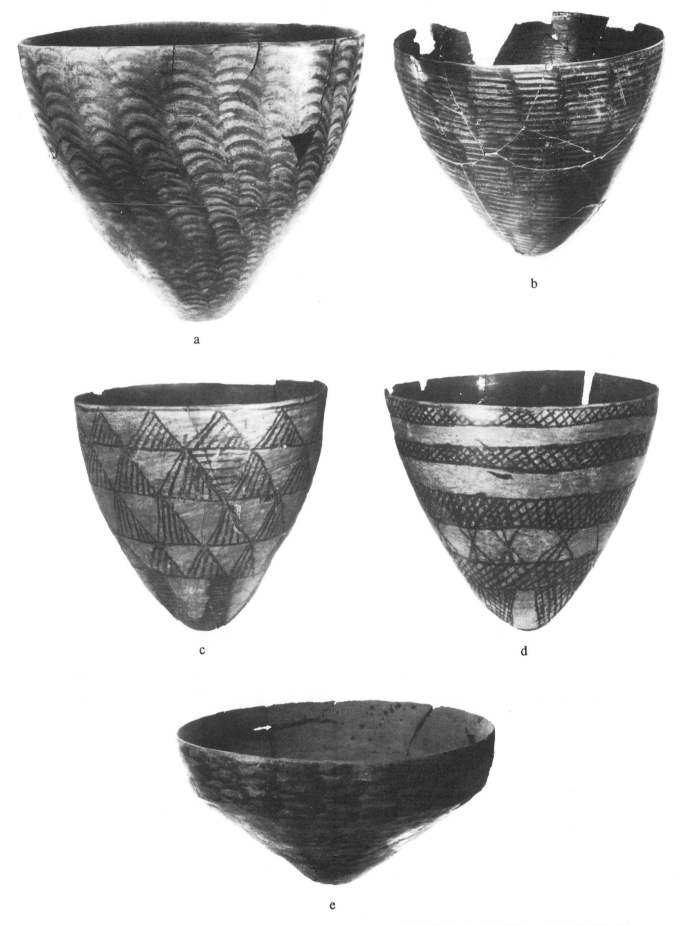

a

b

c

d

e

A-Group Exterior Painted pottery, Form Group I: (a) V 67—15; (b) W 2—1; (c) W 10—1; (d) W 10—13; (e) V 67—22. Scale ca. 2:5.

PLATE 17

A-Group Exterior Painted pottery, Form Group I: (a) V 59—1; (b) W 11—5; (c) S 3 and S 4, sherds. Scale (a) ca. 1:5, (b), (c) ca. 2:5.

PLATE 18

Sherds from Cemetery V: (a) V 65, sherds; (b) V 61, sherds; (c) V 59, sherds. Scale ca. 2:5.

PLATE 19

A-Group Rippled pottery, Form Group II: (a) W 11—9; (b) W 15—4; (c) W 8—2; (d) W 21—1; (e) W 11—15; (f) W 15—5. Scale ca. 2:5.

PLATE 20

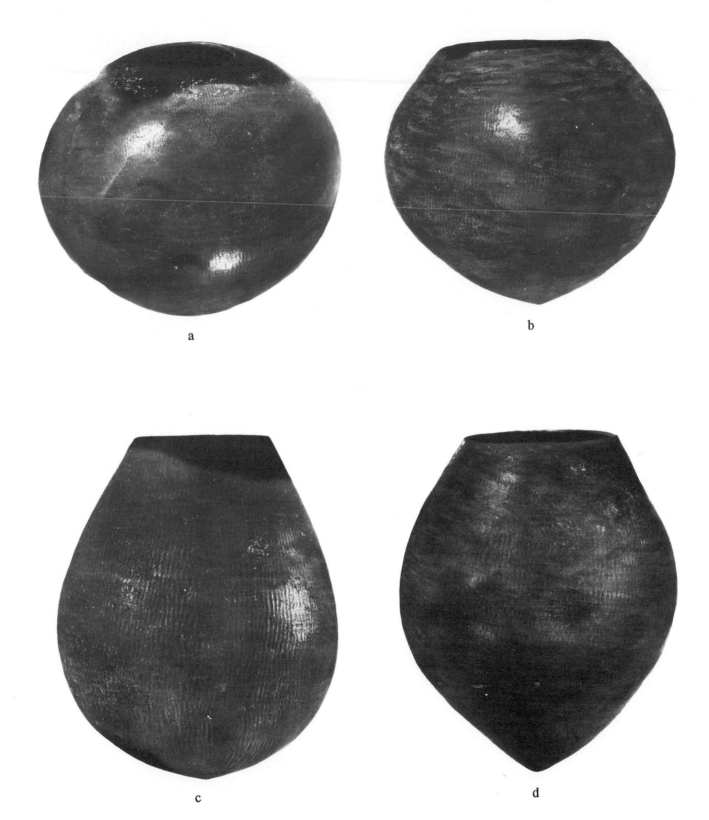

a

b

c

d

A-Group Rippled pottery, Form Group II: (a) Q 631—1; (b) Q 631—2; (c) Q 631—4; (d) Q 631—3. Scale ca. 2:5.

PLATE 21

A-Group Simple Fine pottery, Form Group VI *alpha*: (a) W 2—5; (b) W 11—12; (c) W 19—5; (d) W 19—10; (e) W 2—2; (f) W 6—13. Scale ca. 2:5.

PLATE 22

A-Group ordinary pottery, Form Group VI: Simple Fine pottery, Form Group VI *alpha*— (a) W 10—14; (b) W 32—3; (c) W 32—4; Miniature Cups, Form Group VI *beta*— (d) W 19—3; (e) W 10—21; (f) W 10—23; (g) W 6—16 (also VI *gamma* A2); (h) W 7—3; (i) W 8—3. Scale ca. 2:5.

PLATE 23

A-Group ordinary pottery, Form Group VI: Form Group VI *alpha*— (a) W 15—2 (E2); (b) W 9—2 (E1b); (c) W 27—1 (D); Form Group VI *gamma*— (d) W 32—5; (e) W 6—15; (f) W 6—14; Form Group VI *alpha*— (g) W 25—1 (C2); (h) W 23—2 (D). Scale ca. 2:5.

PLATE 24

A-Group Simple Coarse pottery, Form Group VI *gamma*: (a) W 7—1; (b) W 26—1; (c) W 16—1; (d) W 23—7. Scale ca. 2:5 except (d) ca. 1:3.

PLATE 25

A-Group Simple Coarse pottery, Form Group VI *gamma*: (a) W 11—3; (b) W 5—2. Scale ca. 2:5.

b

a

PLATE 26

Egyptian Hard Pink pottery, Form Group X: (a) W 6—8; (b) W 31—1; (c) W 10—17; (d) W 10—20; (e) W 10—10. Scale ca. 2:5.

PLATE 27

Egyptian Hard Pink pottery, Form Group X; W 10—19. Scale ca. 2:5.

PLATE 28

a

b

c

d

Egyptian Hard Pink pottery, Form Group X: (a) W 10—6; (b) W 22—1; (c) W 19—16; (d) W 6—7.
Scale ca. 2:5.

PLATE 29

Egyptian Hard Pink pottery, Form Group X: (a) W 32—1; (b) W 32—2; (c) W 5—1. Scale ca. 1:5.

PLATE 30

a

b   c

Egyptian Hard Pink pottery, Form Group X: (a) W 19—2; (b) W 10—7; (c) W 11—1. Scale ca. 1:5.

PLATE 31

Egyptian Hard Pink pottery, Form Group X: (a) W 10—5; (b) W 11—2. Scale ca. 1:5.

PLATE 32

a

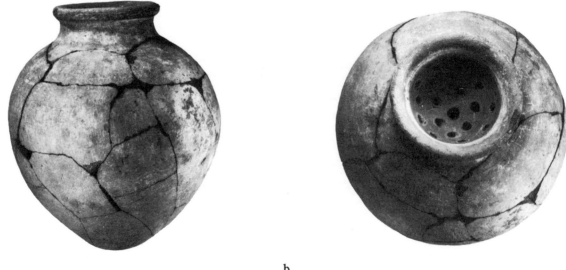

b

Egyptian pottery: (a) Hard Pink jar, Form Group X, W 6—5; (b) Coarse strainer jar, Form Group XI, W 19—1. Scale ca. 1:5.

PLATE 33

A bowl of A-Group VI *alpha*, made in a shape of Egyptian Hard Pink pottery, painted outside with trees and inside with spiral lines: W 11—8. Scale ca. 1:2.

PLATE 34

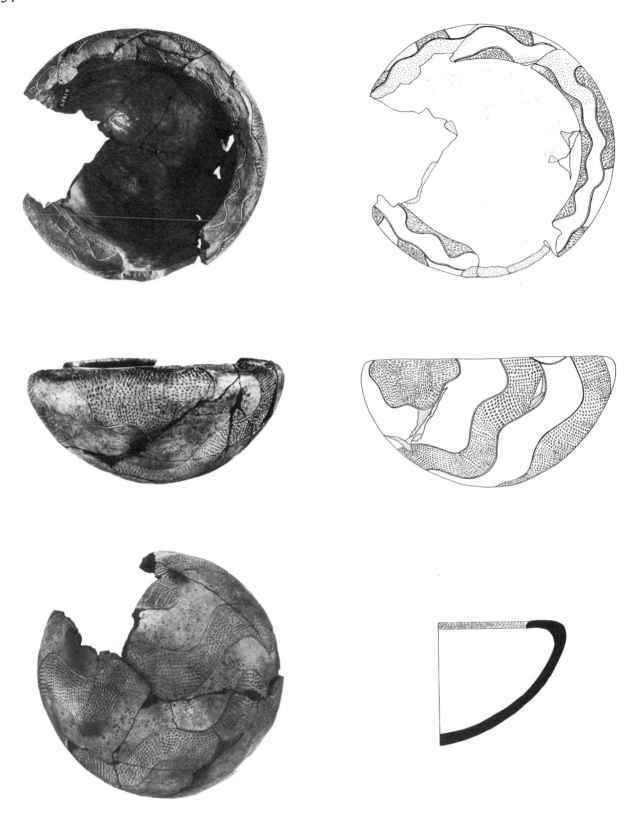

A Heavy Incised bowl of Form Group VIII: V 67—23. Scale 2:5

PLATE 35

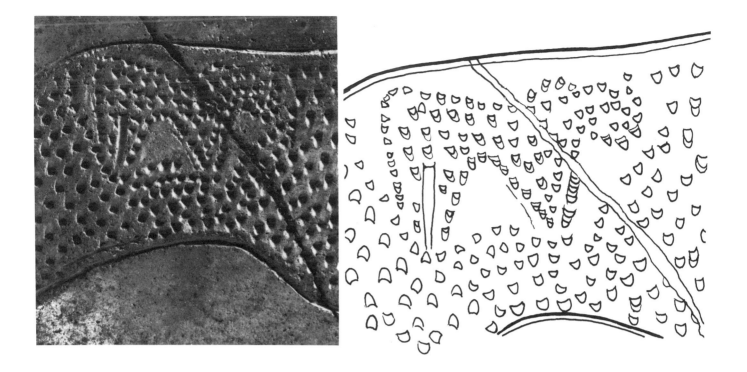

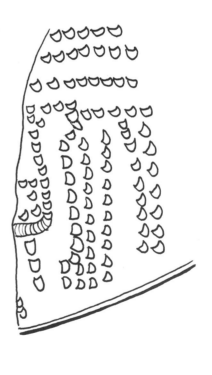

A Heavy Incised bowl of Form Group VIII; drawings and photographs of animal figures: V 67—23.

PLATE 36

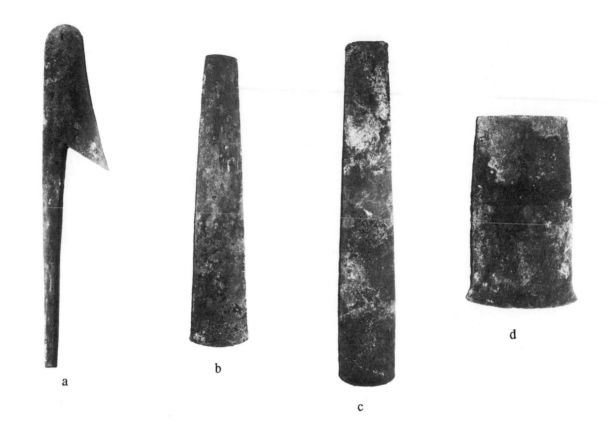

Copper tools and weapons from W 11; a mortar and pestle from W 19. (a) Harpoon, W 11—16; (b) Adze, W 11—19; (c) Adze, W 11—18; (d) Axe, W 11—17; (e) Mortar and Pestle, W 19—7. Scale ca. 1:2 except (e) ca. 1:4

PLATE 37

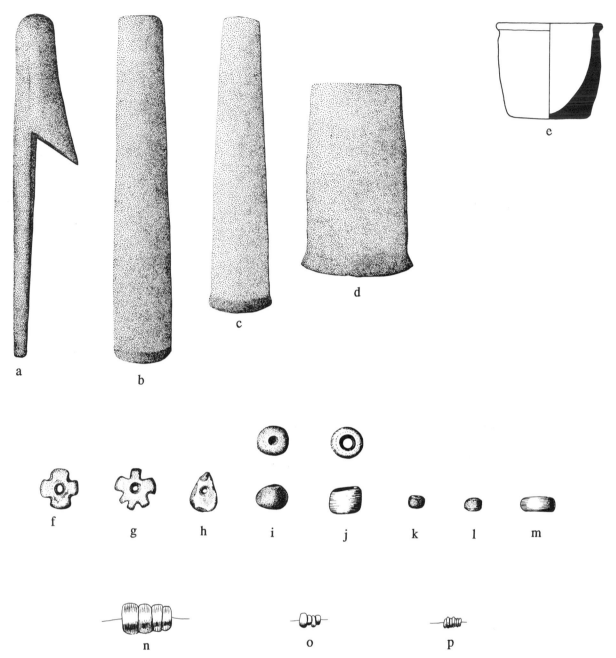

A-Group objects: Copper tools and weapons— (a) Harpoon, W 11—16; (b) Adze, W 11—19; (c) Adze, W 11—18; (d) Axe, W 11—17; (e) Stone jar, S 1—4; Beads: (f-g) Notched faience beads, W 22—2f; (h) Rock crystal pendant, W 22-2h; (i) Faience ball bead, T 75-2; (j) Tooth barrel bead, W 22-2b; (k-l) Faience discoid beads, W 19—9c; (m) Tooth discoid bead, W 11—23; (n) Discoid stone beads, W 22—2a, c, and g; (o) Discoid stone beads, W 19—9a, b; (p) Discoid faience beads, T243—1. Scale (a), (b), (c), (d), (e) 1:2, (f), (g), (h), (i), (j), (k), (l), (m), (n), (o), (p) 1:1.

PLATE 38

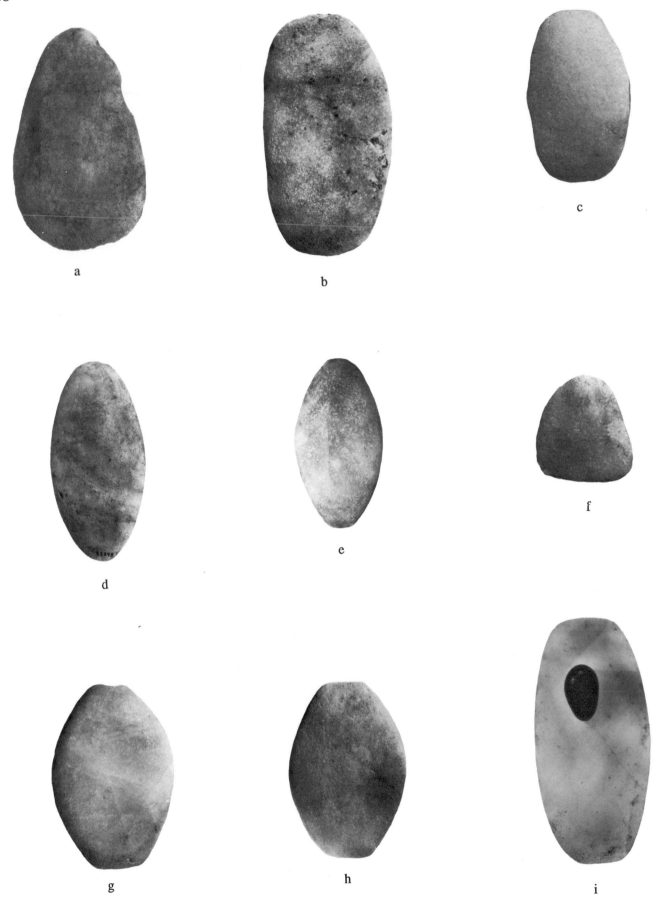

Palettes: (a) W 7—5; (b) W 33—2; (c) W 6—11; (d) W 2—7; (e) W 2—4; (f) W 2—8; (g) W 6—9; (h) W 5—4; (i) W 11—11. Scale ca. 1:2.

PLATE 39

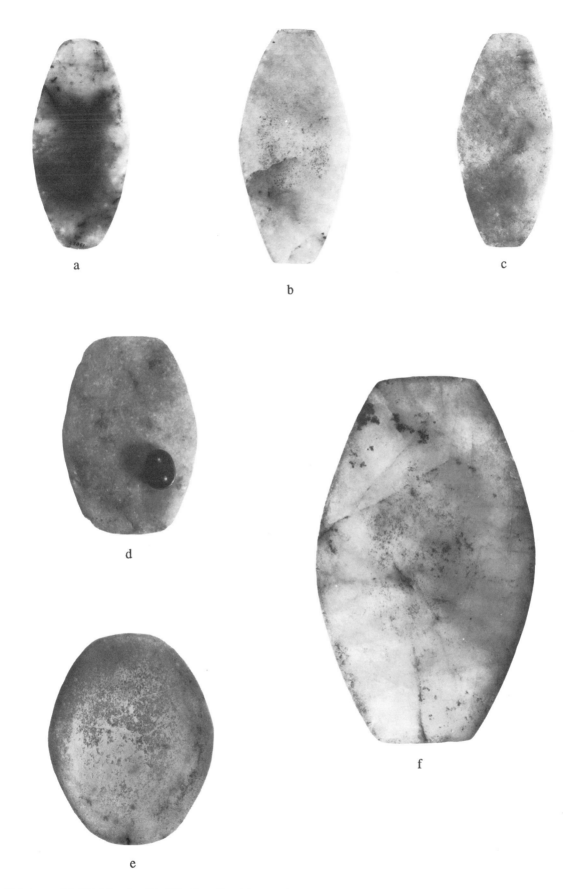

Palettes: (a) W 19—8; (b) W 19—13; (c) W 10—16; (d) W 9—1; (e) W 38—3; (f) W 11—20. Scale ca. 1:2.

PLATE 40

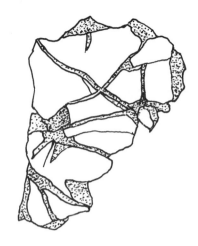

A cake of resin or incense from V 67—9a. Scale ca. 1:1.

PLATE 41

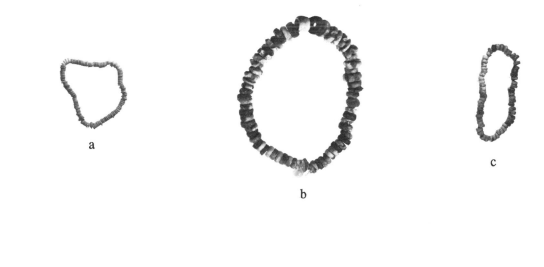

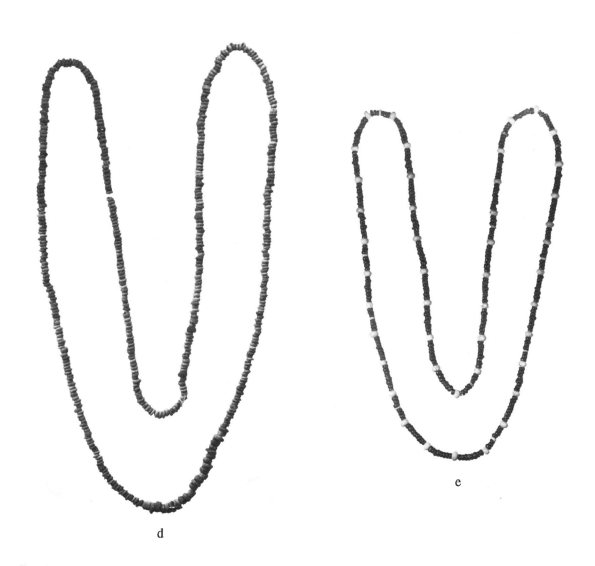

Beads: (a) W 20—1; (b) W 22—2; (c) W 11—23; (d) W 29—1; (e) W 19—9. Scale ca. 1:2 except (c) ca. 1:4.

PLATE 42

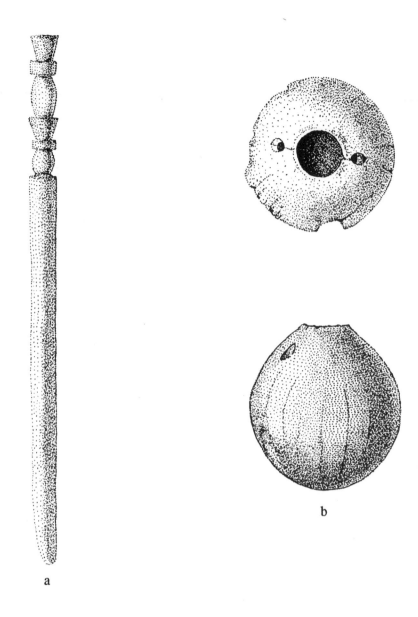

a

b

Ivory objects from S 3: (a) No. 6; (b) No. 7. Scale 1:1.

PLATE 43

A-Group objects: (a) Ivory jar fragment, S 3—8; (b) Ivory jar, S 3—7; (c) Ivory pin, S 3—6; (d) Clay model of incense cake (?), W 6—10. Scale ca.1:1 except (d) ca. 1:2.

PLATE 44

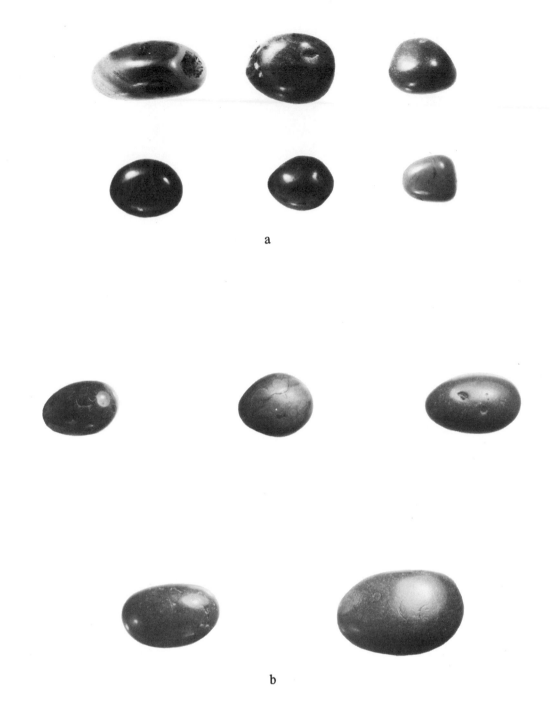

Pebbles: (a) W 32—6; (b) W 6—17. Scale ca. 1:1.

PLATE 45

a

b

The cave east of Cemetery K; location and entrance.

PLATE 46

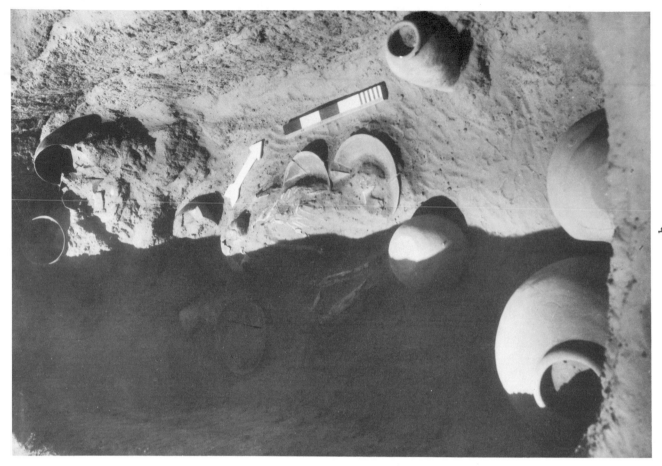

b

a

(a) W 6 and (b) W 10.

PLATE 47

(a) W 21 and (b) W 19.

b

a

PLATE 48

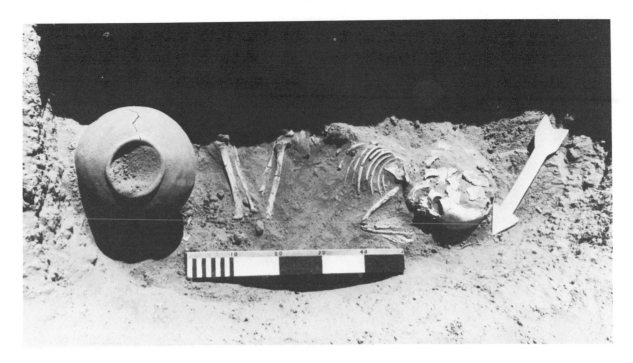

a

b

(a) W 26 and (b) W 23.

PLATE 49

(a) W 32 and (b) W 31.

b

a

PLATE 50

(a) W 86 and (b) Q 631.

b

a

PLATE 51

T 155.

PLATE 52

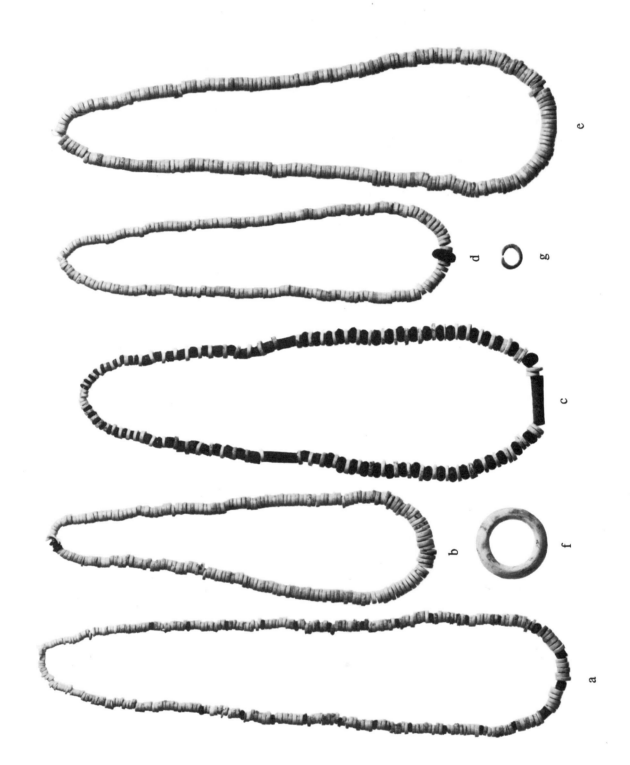

Jewelry from T 155: (a) Bracelet of ostrich egg beads, no. 10; (b) Anklet of ostrich egg beads, no. 12; (c) Necklace of ostrich egg and one faience bead, no. 11; (d) Bracelet of ostrich egg and blue faience beads, no. 14; (e) Anklet of ostrich egg beads, no. 13; (f) Shell ring, no. 9; (g) Shell earring or hair-ring, no. 15. Scale ca. 3:4.

PLATE 53

Objects from T 35 and a mirror from T 155: Red-polished Egyptian jars— (a) T 35—2; (b) T 35—1;
(c) Copper axe, T 35—4; (d) Copper mirror, T 155—5. Scale (a), (b) ca. 2:5, (c) ca. 1:1, (d) ca. 1:2.

PLATE 54

Objects from T 155: (a) Small Egyptian jar, no. 1; (b) Pebbles, no. 7; (c) Fragments of malachite, no. 2; (d) Copper awl or kohl stick, no. 6; (e) Palette and grinding-pebble, no. 8; (f) Grindstone or palette and pestle, nos. 3-4. Scale ca. 1:2 except (a) ca. 2:5.

PLATE 55

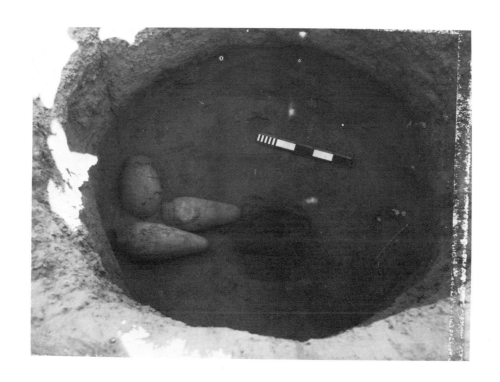

Storage Pit Q 80.